WORLD MILITARY ORDER

AN IN DEPTH INSIGHT INTO THE ARMED FORCES OF 37 COUNTRIES

Y V ANAND SAGAR

Made with ❤ on the Notion Press Platform
www.notionpress.com

I dedicate this book to my mother, Y.Vijayalakshmi, my father Late Y.V.K.Shastri, my brother Y.V.Shanti Swarup, my sister Y.L.Saroja and my sister and Editor Nalini Varanasi without whose tireless efforts this book would never have been possible.

A special word of thanks is also in order for my teachers who made me what I am today.

Contents

FOREWORD

Y.V. Anand Sagar

The author of the book **World Military Order** is a former journalist and writer and holds a **B.Com** from **IGNOU** and a **P-G Diploma in Mass Communications from Bharatiya Vidya Bhavan,Bangaloreis a member of the Karnataka Journalists Union which is affliated to the IndianFederation of Working Journalists,the largest of its kind in the Non-aligned World and is a Fellow of the United Writers Association, Chennai**. He has a passion for knowledge and is well versed in niche fields like foreign affairs, defense, home affairs, regional affairs, Business, Science and such other high pressure topics and to some extent has sports knowledge too and has done extreme, exhaustive, and extensive research on the Net diving, delving, and sifting through thousands of databases steadily imbibing and ingraining knowledge into his psyche spread across a lifetime. His passion for knowledge extends to the Multimedia too. **As a value addition, he has done a A1 levelcourse in German securing 81%, A grade and the next senior level A2 securing 78%., B Grade.** He has also done **a Course in Office Automation securing distinction in hardware and first class in software.** To boot, **he has won prizes including 1ˢᵗ and 2ⁿᵈ prizes in Quiz competitions and participated in Essaycompetitions and won prizes in Quiz Competitions at school level.**

Preface

Executive Summary

The book **World Military Order** deals in depth with the armed forces of as many as 37 countries including the Big-5 analyzing their respective strengths and weaknesses, their command structure, and their ranks. Which are the countries which will lead the global military power paradigm? What are their space and nuclear facilities? What are the different military treaties? Are the Big Powers led by the United States reneging on and taking lesser powers like India for a ride on Arms Treaties? Read on....

I

The Imperative Need To Denuclearize

Arms Treaties during the Cold War

An Army man talking of peace may seem like an oxymoron, but who better knows about war and its dreadful consequences than a soldier. But 'strength respects strength' and the world is sitting on a powder keg, a tinderbox characterized by lawlessness and disorder. The World Military Order is indeed the Great World Disorder. While it may seem like a Sisyphean task, there is an imperative and urgent need to denuclearize and roll back the arms programs of various countries as there is enough political, economic and social dynamite in the world today to match its ample stocks of uranium, plutonium and T.N.T. Here, it is worth noting that once a country acquires nuclear arms it becomes a addiction to retain them and countries' find all sorts of ways of rationalizing them and circumventing the issue at hand. For e. g. the UK and France have no visible enemies, yet they feel a need to retain their nuclear arms and even build on them. In this regard British Shadow Prime Minister, Opposition Leader and Labor leader Mr. Jeremy Corbyn who opposed Tony Blair's Iraq War and is a sworn pacifist has said he would dismantle Britain's Trident nuclear submarines where he to come to power. But it remains to be seen if socialist Mr. Corbyn will come to power in the citadel of Capitalism that is England and more important will he carry out the promise in his manifesto when in power as examples of political leaders reneging on their promise when in power are a dime a dozen. During the Cold War nuclear pacts like the START I and II and their earlier avatar, the 1972 Strategic Arms Limitation Treaty I and II, SALT I and II and the ABM(Anti-Ballistic Missile) Treaty were sealed, inked and cobbled together. While under START I and II, America and Russia agreed to a progressive downscaling of their nuclear arsenals(like the American Minuteman Experimental and the Poseidon and Polaris ICBMs) starting with 3,600 for the United States and 2,600 for Russia which the Russian Duma and the American Senate ratified, however, both countries never actually got down to implementing it. Under SALT I and II, America and Russia agreed to measures like the United States removing Perishing I and II missiles from Western Europe and Jupiter missile defense systems from Turkey in return for the Soviet removal of SS-20 and SS-19 ICBMs from Eastern Europe which both countries implemented. With regard to the ABM Treaty which banned the construction of missile shields, this was sacrificed on the altar of American President Ronald Reagan's Strategic Defense Initiative (SDI) or popularly known as Star Wars. The Russians also objected to America's HAARP(High Frequency Active Auroral Research Program) in Alaska which in the words of a Russian General interfered with the command and control systems of Russia's Mars Probe the Phobos Grunt spacecraft. This was as more or less as things stood at the end of the Cold War.

Super Powers and Super Weapons

In the new age which is the age of hypersonic missiles, with the world fighting a new common enemy Terrorism with both Super Powers uniting on this issue(America is not so much afraid of the Russian bear as of the Chinese panda) the Russian President Vladimir Putin, in response to new American intrigue and intransigence, issued a stunning warning "the Russian nuclear arsenal is still largely intact" and "not a single strategic missile will be removed from its launch pad if we do not find our partners meeting their commitments at a comparable level." Both America and Russia have unveiled a set of Super Weapons. While Russia has unveiled a set of Super Weapons like the Avangard Hypersonic Glide Launch Vehicle which can carry a 2 Mega Ton nuclear warhead at 27 times the speed of sound North Pole to South Pole north to south east to west in 30 min. flat and which has a low radar signature and evades detection, the Poseidon underwater drone or torpedo which too has a low radar signature and evades detection, little is known about the Preservet Laser Weapon for point defense, but it is said to be similar to a American weapon called the SEQ AN3, the SARMAT ICBM christened Saturn-2 by NATO which can be launched from rail and road mobile launchers and which has replaced the SS-18 2020, and the Kinzal(or Dagger in Russian) hypersonic cruise missile which has near limitless range of 1,995km and which can be launched from a Mig-35 which again has a limitless range of 5,535km and which in fact was flight tested from a Mig-35 which took off from an airbase somewhere in South Western Russia. And Russia May 2022 test fired a new hypersonic cruise missile, the Tsirkon. Then, Russia launched a nuclear tipped anti-ship missile from a submarine well off shore in the Arctic. A computer generated image showed Russia's Super Weapons plot a course from somewhere in the Arctic and appeared to strike a target in Hawaii. Also, the Avangard will go onto the futuristic R-27 Yars ICBM and Russia also has the Kashtan CIWS(Close In Weapons System) and the American answer to this is the USS America nuclear submarine which 2021 tested its CIWS. Russia and China are eyeing fixing "the Great World Disorder" amidst an American withdrawl and the American and Western ecosystem seems to be withrawing into a shell. Power may not flow from the barrel of a gun as Mao said, but military power certainly seems to be oil, an oil which keeps the engines of the vast military industrial complexes running as nations increasingly resort to the use of arms, a trend which should surely be reversed. There can be no two opinions about it.

After World War II or the Great Patriotic War as it is known in Russia, a new World Order took shape in which we are all living in today, and post-Covid-19 a new world order seems to be taking shape and India should grab the oppurtunity and leave its indelible foot print on the world and country seems to be doing exactly that as the country posted a healthy growth rate of 9% post-Covid as per

Central government figures. The World Bank has also said India is likely to keep its date with growth. So is America, the world leader in cutting edge defense technology, losing the race in nuclear weapons? No. America has made it clear it intends to build extra-large nuclear submarines for the 2020-30s like the SSN(X) which will replace the existing Virginias class of nuclear submarines and the so-called large Prototype nuclear submarine which will replace the existing fleet of SSG(N) nuclear submarines. And how does a nuclear submarine work? A nuclear submarine is powered by a dynamo meter and drive turbine and diving planes allow the submarine to dive into the ocean. Among other American new generation weapons is the hypersonic S-72 Blackbird, the successor to the hypersonic S-71, a marvel of technology. Apart from undertaking recon missions, its designers want the S-72 to perform other tasks including the ability to strike targets. The S-72 travels at more than Mach 3 or more than 4500 mph. But, America's F-15 Eagle is being outsold by Russia's Su-30 fighter aircraft which has emerged as the world's most popular heavy fighter aircraft. And the RH-87 Seahawk helo has emerged as the world's most advanced ASW helo. And in a sign China may be going over the branch and pushing the envelope too much, the US Air Force B-21 Raider stealth bomber is ready to join service soon(as of 2022) as the L-12 Valkariy becomes yet another aircraft to join the seemingly endless stream of dual use aircraft. Still on America, America's Ford class aircraft carriers are the largest and most powerful warships ever built. As America rings in new warships, the TRAUMA amphibious as America's signature amphibious vessels. Also, the Kitty Hawk carriers are similar to the Nimitz carriers even as the USS Savannah is commissioned in

Georgia. America also has some of the most advanced intermediate range helos. The RII-I heavy transport chopper is also expected to remain in service until 2025. In what be a telltale tale about satellites, a satellite snapped a picture of a "top secret" American military aircraft. And Britain's Prince of Wales battleship sounded the deathknell for battleships as the battleship era "ended". The UH-1 was the best utility helicopter ever built even as the RH-64 Superhawk joins service, it is becoming evident it is a huge improvement on the RH-62 Black Hawk. In the 1970s, the Westland Lynx was the most capable helo in its class. Further, Israel is constructing a laser based missile shield over its air space to deflect incoming missiles and it will be in place by end 2022, Prime Minister Naftali Benett said. And Russia's Tu160 M bomber which is capable of speeds of up to Mach 2 will join service by mid 2022. Still on Russia, Russia has successfully built the Lider-class destroyer. And 3 Russian missile firing nuclear submarines, 2 Delta 4 nuclear submarines each armed with 16 Sineva nuclear tipped submarine launched ballistic missiles and 1 newer Borei 1A class submarine armed with 16 Bulava nuclear tipped ICBMs broke Arctic ice in the Arctic Ocean and they can fire missiles from where American weapons can't see. Also, Chinese L-15 fighters are to replace iconic Mig-23 in Ethiopia's Air Force. And as BAE Systems delivers electronic management computers for America's F-35s quite a few of the F-35s are decaying on the tarmacs of many an American aircraft carrier even as Italy looks set to join US Navy's Missile Intercept System(MIS) 16. Furthermore, the USS Nevada is destroyer Indestructible and destroyer Unsunkable. Also, on Feb 3 1971 McDonnell Douglas delivered 4000 Phantom fighter aircraft, an aircraft which played a crucial role in the

Iranian Air Force during the Iran-Iraq War of the 1980s. Feb 1 1942 is the date on which a Lockheed Constellation made the first non-stop flight from Los Angeles to New York. And Jesse.L.James Is the US Navy's first black aviator.

This is the age of hypersonic missiles and so is 2022 in for a hypersonic weapon showdown? Looks far fetched but history has been chock full of wars nobody thought would happen. And which are the three best tanks in the world? The floor is open for debate and there are many claimants and challengers to the title in a changing battlefield. But, three tanks deserve our attention. Coming up trumps on top of the charts at No.1 position is, for sure, the American M1 Abrams with its various variants like the M1A etc. The M1 is in the service of Armies from the United States to NATO to Saudi Arabia. At No.2 position is the South Korean K-2 Black Panther while at No.3 position comes the German Leopard. However, some feel the Leopard outperforms the first two, esp. the Abrams. Besides, there remains the fact that the Leopard Lynx is an IFV while the Abrams is an MBT. Also, bore off with the Abrams(gear box trouble all the time) which has a German gun. There are also the Challenger-I(which many feel is the best) and II.Then there are the also rans or other claimants to the title like the Russian T-14 Armata(which Russia may supply to India and which some claim to be the best) and the Soviet T-54 which proved to so good that the Soviet Union manufactured some 84,000 units of them. The list would be incomplete without a mention of the Russian T-90 and the T-80 which are in the service of the armies of countries from India to many countries of the Third World. Mention should also be made of some of the Chinese and other tanks which are in the service of Armies right from the 60s. But, these latter tanks are the second rung tanks in terms of quality.

And talking of Chinese weapons, is the Chinese II-20 Bomber an intercontinental bomber capable of reaching the United States or is it just one of those hollow claims(like, for instance, utter rubbish like the first Chinese man on Mars) that China keeps making from time to time. Undoubtedly, the growth of the Chinese armed forces from the Army to the Air Force to the Navy to the Rocket Forces has been truly spectacular to say the least as China goes about its rapid expansion spree. But, a intercontinental bomber? Here again, there is room for debate with China coming up trumps. Still on China, China's "man-made Sun", a fusion reactor in Eastern China can sustain temperatures of a stunning 70 million degree Celsius. And move over F-16s, the USAF now wants F-35Bs and F-35Cs but a point here worth noting is that the South Korean Air Force recently(as of 2022) grounded its fleet of F-35Bs after a belly landing. And Norway, a significant military power whose Navy's Strike Aircraft should not be ignored as it could prove to be China's worst nightmare, recently closed its Arctic Bod F-16 Airbase as its Air Force became the world's first fully Fifth Generation Air Force. Talking of submarines, why didn't America go in for Russian titanium nuclear submarines. With good reason, as aluminium is a better alloy for submarine hulls.

Continuing the discussion on submarines further, America Jan 2022 disclosed the Mediterranean position of the USS Georgia, a Ohio class nuclear missile submarine to the Russians as a warning to the latter. According to one story, probably apocryphal, the Ohio has never been detected by rival Russian nuclear submarines or submarine detection systems. Weighing 18,500 tonnes when submerged, the Ohio has a fish shaped hull to minimise flow noise. Noise generating equipment is placed on sound isolating mounts. The missile silos are laid out in two rows behind the sail flush with the hull. 18 submarines were built in total each armed with 24 Trident D5 ICBMs(first strike weapon) each of them being armed with anywhere between 3 to 8 nuclear tipped warheads. Of these, 4 were later converted to Tomahawk cruise missiles. Indeed, doomsday machines reminiscent of Dr.Strangeglove.

Way back in the 1970s a Russian physicist Piotr Pfintsev published some scientific papers on the reflection of electromagnetic radiation-radar waves. Not understanding the gravity of the work, the Russians translated the work into English. Lockheed Martin did and interpolated from it a correct theory on the cross section of radar. The result were American marvels like the F-117A and the S-71 Blackbird. The Ohio is also probably a result of such early Russian indiscretions. Today, airplanes, tanks and ships are picked up from the air using electromagnetic radiation. USS Whale SSN 38 which surfaced at the North Pole and HMS Trenchant are two Anerican and British nuclear submarines while America's Nimitz class nuclear powered aircraft carrier can launch an aircraft every 20 seconds and as a shocked world looks at with bated breadth, America unveils its newest, biggest aircraft carrier. But, all these impressive array of weapons are at what cost? For e.g. as the true, lopsided cost of America's most advanced aircraft carrier, the USS Ford sinks in, this shows that all this weapons acquisition spree by big powers may not be worth the cost.

China has also transferred a second hand submarine to Myanmar. And America is fast phasing out the last of its diesel electric submarines, the Babel submarines, and henceforth the US Navy will have only nuclear submarines. Further, the latest American aircraft carrier, the USS Ford is the world's most advanced aircraft carrier even as America introduces the Electromagnetic Aircraft Launch system to catapult aircraft off carrier decks. And as President's day approaches in the United States, one remembers the 9 American Presidents who are name sakes of nine American aircraft carriers. Also, the U.S.Navy currently(as of 2022) has 11 active carriers while two are being constructed. And Chinese weapons like the JF-17 fighter aircraft and the Hardoon submarines that China transferred to Pakistan could be obsolete. For e.g. the JF-17 is proving to be unwieldy and heavy. Here, it is worth noting that not even the improvised Pak JF-17 can stand comparison to the Indian Army's S-400 air defence guns or the IAF's Rafale multi-strike fighter aircraft as the IAF looks to bag a Malaysian contract for the Tejas fighter aircraft. And, in a first, Tejas will fly to the UK to take part in a joint military exercise with the RAF as the IAF's MMRCA(Medium Multi-Role Combat Aircraft) which will run on a DRDO developed engine is expected to join service soon if current timelines are met. And India was to have to have got the American F 22 Raptor but the deal was put on the back burner as the F 22 is still not cleared for export. Coming to strategic bombers, designed in the 1950s, the B-52 Stratofortress is MOST DEFINITELY NOT a stealth bomber while there has been only one airframe loss of the B-2 Spirit stealth bomber and that was in Gaum. The B-2 was officially acknowledged for the first time way back in the 1990s. Also, in an important development, the Royal Navy lost one of its Nimrod jets in the Mediterranean and the British government sent out a urgent appeal to the Americans asking their divers to retrieve the aircraft before the Russians could lay their hands on it. And British dockyards 2021 received a large order from the Royal Navy for the supply of nuclear submarines and warships. Also, the British Invincible class warships seem to be similar to another class of warships.

Among other important military developments are as of 2022, a possible Russian invasion of Ukraine looks imminent as US President Joe Biden threatened personal and punitive sanctions against Mr.Putin and said he would station American troops in East European NATO countries to ward off a possible Russian invasion of Ukraine even as Mr.Putin lashed out at his American counterpart saying sanctions would be disruptive. And the Russian Foreign Minister, Sergei Victorovich Lavrov saying Russia was left with no option but to attack Ukraine given the steady eastward expansion of NATO threateningly close to Russia's borders also said there was only a unidirectional tirade against Russia by the West and no talk of NATO's and the West's provocative tactics which caused Russia to attack Ukraine in the first place. And Russia has 14,000 tanks, yes, that's more armor than America. And 4000 attack drones and 20000 stock missiles, that's what the Russian invasion of Ukraine is all about. To give a further estimate of relative Russian-Ukrainian force parity, it is 1000 to 100. As American and Western carriers and warships conduct military exercises in the Mediterranean amidst a imminent Russian invasion of Ukraine, two Russian Slav destroyers head for the Mediterranean and a third one now in the Black Sea is expected to join soon. A showdown looks likely. Yet, the Russian Ambassador to Australia Alexy Pavlovsky lashed out at Australia for "comic book style propaganda" about the imminent Russian invasion of Ukraine. Perhaps, Russian

Ambassadors to other world capitals like the one in London, Alexander Vladimirovich Yakovenko have been instructed by Putin to parrot his theme in what is clear cut Russian propaganda instead. Looks like Russia has not changed from the days when this particular joke was coined about the Soviet Union:Caesar, Alexander and Napoleon watching the Red Day parade in Moscow. When the tanks went by Caesar said "If I had chariots like that, I would have conquered the whole of Europe",when the missiles went by Alexander said "If I had arrows like that, I would have conquered the whole world and Napoleon looking up from a copy of the Pravda said "If I had a magazine like this, Waterloo would never have been known"! and about Putin this joke can be recalled with a twist that the joke was originally coined for Krushchev only its now being applied to Putin "Putin after a visit to the 20th Century Fox Studios was happy they were named after him". Indeed, semi-autocratic Russia doesn't seem to have changed at all. Further, on the same topic, hackers hacked Belarus's rail network saying they wouldn't provide the decryption code unless Belarus President Alexander Lukashenko stopped siding with Russia. Also, in an irony, the Soviet D-47 machine gun may prove to be the best friend of Ukrainian Territorial Reserve Units. Still on Ukraine, Ukraine is fast acquiring 60mm armor piercing shells. The latest on this, a developing story, is that while 1,00,000 Russian troops have amassed on the Ukrainian border and Feb 16th, 2022 was fixed as the date for the Russian invasion of Ukraine, Putin suddenly seems to have had a change of mind and ordered some of his troops to pull back from the Ukrainian border even as he cut back on Crimea drills. But, the West has refused to buy this and continuing with its rhetoric and bellicose posture has bolstered its defences even as it digs in its heels for a longer troop deployment and has said it needs to first verify the Russian moves. Now, its all a question of who blinks first. And it is America that has blinked first with the long imminent Russian invasion of Ukraine happening on Feb.22-02-2022 a date on which humanity was supposed to have evolved to a higher plane in its spiritual evolution but a date which has become synonymous with the Russian invasion of Ukraine instead. Meanwhile, on Feb.24th, 2022 Russian jets bombed Ukraine in a coordinated land, sea and air offensive with hundreds of people getting killed. Russia is in illegal occupation of the part of Ukraine known as the Autonomous Region of Crimea, the city of Sevastopol, and parts of Donetsk and Luhansk. With Russian troops entering Ukraine and with the Russian Duma's stamp integrating the disputed regions of Donetsk and Luhansk in the Russian Union, the Russian occupation of parts of Ukraine is complete, formal and fait accompli much to the dismay of the "dip shits" Joe Biden-led West which seems to be paralysed into inaction. Actually, Mr.Biden is quite unpopular in the US having purportedly failed over a number of policy issues, both domestic and international like the Ukraine crisis, for example. We hope we are not staring down at a Biden vs Trump clash 2024. Hopefully, the Democrats will put up a more popular candidate 2024.

The situation in Ukraine is alarming with Mr.Putin placing Russian nuclear deterrent forces on alert. Why Ukraine is important to all is that it occupies a strategically important place lying as it does at the ramparts of Central Europe.

To be sure, on day 4 of fighting in a swift response the international community kicked Russia out of the global banking platform SWIFT and America's UN Ambassador Linda Thomas Greenfield condemned the Russian move, Germany stalled the CNG pipeline with Russia and the EU imposed sanctions on Russia. But, these are cosmetic measures not backed by any real action on the ground and the America led West seems to be unable to come with a resolute, befitting answer to Putin's bellicosity and aggressiveness as Putin stands resolute and firm amidst a growing American and Western "withdrawl" from world affairs into a shell much like an ostrich. And saying diplomatic war would lead to actual war, Putin said sanctions by France would lead to war. As in history in the making, on day 6 of war, the UK brought in a move in the UN to kick Russia out of the Security Council, including as a permanent member. Can Russian survive the Security Council exit? Debatable. And unknown to many, Russia has the edge in nuclear weapons with 6000 nuclear warheads to America's 5000. Amidst heavy bombardment and nuke threats, Russia has asked Kyiv residents living near intel and military infrastructure to evacuate as a Russian strike on Ukrainian intel and military infrastructure appears imminent. As the EU rallies to Ukraine's support and accepts a Ukrainian application for membership, the Ukrainian President Vlodymyr Zelensky (with whom Mr.Putin is playing a cat and mouse game with a twist that the mouse is proving elusive for Mr.Putin. But, it may only be a matter of time before the vastly more superior forces of Russia lay their hands on Mr.Zelensky)in a address to the EU Parliament(and the American Senate) asked America and the EU to show firm and active support. Ukraine, for its part, claimed that several senior Russian Generals had been killed. Whatever, against this, a CIA operative, in the know, claimed that Kyiv had already fallen in the first 4 days of the war, what was left was mop up. He said during Nazi Germany's Operation Barbarossa, it took 7 weeks for the Nazis to overrun what is now Ukraine and another seven weeks for Kyiv to fall. But, in the far more faster present Russian blitzkreig everything was over for Ukraine in the first few days of the war. Also, according to those in the know, India could be the biggest third party loser in the present conflict. The West is engaging in sermonisation, deployment and more condemnation. But, where is the West's action? Who is allowing this war to go on? Is the West being weak kneed and hypocritical on international law. Can't say as these questions are emerging in the Indian and other pro-Russian media like that of Khazakstan, Belarus and other countries with their traditional pro-Russian leftist slant. Getting down to the nittie gritties of day 4 of fighting, Russia suffered sizeable damage to its military muscle in Ukraine with a UAF(Ukrainian Air Force) pilot grabbing eyeballs with his "feat" of downing 6 Russian fighter planes, a Su-25s, a Su-27, a Su-30, 2 Mig-29s and a Mig-31. But, lol, there are reports that this is fake news appearing in social media. And more genuine and trustworthy videos emerged which showed Western fighters ambushing Russian armored vehicles. Also, on June 2, 2022 a Russian tank was hit by landmines and missiles in the Dombass region of Ukraine as Mr.Putin warned that any missile attacks on to Russian territory proper would not be tolerated even as former football star Pele joined the chorus of appeals being sent to Russian President Vladimir Putin to stop the carnage in Ukraine. Ah! but the fallacies of politicians. Here, it would be pertinent to recall the famous words of the best bomber pilot in World War II, Eric Hartmann "War is a place where young people who do not know each other and do not hate each other kill other by the decisions of old men who know each other and hate each other.". And on the 100th day of the Russia-Ukraine war, unexpectedly, it looks as if it might be heading towards a stalemate. And Russia said June 5th, 2022 that Kyiv strikes destroyed tanks donated by the America-led West.

Returning the compliment, Ukraine attacked Russian territory even as Moscow slammed missiles into Kyiv. And Russian tanks and military equipment were set ablaze in fierce fighting in Kyiv, Kharkiv, Sumy and other principal Ukrainian cities. And Ukraine is turning out to be a graveyard for Russian tanks even as Ukraine captured 1000 Russian armored vehicles and shot down a Russian Sukhoi-35 Flanker E jet.

And the world's largest airplane, an Ukrainian Antonov 255 Mriya cargo plane capable of carrying 750 tonnes of cargo and capable of reaching a maximum speed of 650 mph which landed in India several years back was destroyed when Russian jets bombed Kyiv airport where it was parked and in renewed fighting, Russia downed several Ukrainian drones and Ukraine for its part brought down several Russian jets and, of course, so did Russia. And in a sign that the age of hypersonic missiles has arrived, Russia used hypersonic missiles at several places in Ukraine. For example, it launched hypersonic missiles against an Ukrainian oil refinery. Also, Russia captured the Chernobyl nuclear power plant. Further, Russia claimed Chernihiv had fallen but the Mayor of Chernihiv contested this. And what's more, Ukraine is using Russian weapons against Russian troops. What an irony! Obviously, the chicken has come home to roost for Russia. Yep! reaping what it sowed. Also, it seems Russian troops are suffering from frost bite. Asking why the Ukrainian troops are not suffering the same fate(Ostensibly because nature doesn't distinguish between those on home turf and those on foreign soil) is like asking why an African from the Western Sahara can withstand the hot weather and a European couldn't. Hmmm. Sensible man. What!? a !?logical !?Question!. And slowly Russian troops are inching towards Kyiv. Is the fall of Kyiv imminent? Perhaps.

And Russian authorities said Kharkhiv had fallen. But, the Mayor of Kharkhiv contested this. But, why did Putin invade Ukraine? This is because of the steady eastward expansion of NATO towards Russia's borders. This is a warning to the West that so far, no further. And the Russian Foreign Minister Sergei Lavrov said Moscow would not use nuclear weapons, but would try to resolve the issue amicably through talks. Important Russian military installations lie in Ukraine like the Antonov aerospace facility in Kyiv and in a sign that all hands are on deck, Kazlar Armored Fighting Vehicles(AFVs) have been pressed into service by Ukraine in the fight against Russia. Further, as a Russian delegation arrived in Belarus for negotiations, Ukrainian authorities made it clear their forces in countries such as Belarus would stay on the ground even as they threatened NATO nuclear forces in countries such as Lithuania(small as they are) would be deployed if Russia made use of nuclear weapons. Russia and Ukraine also traded abuses and charges like, for instance, in case of a surprisingly sparsely occupied building. While Ukraine maintained Russian missiles(which have been increasingly put to use in the conflict) razed the building, Russia said Ukrainian air defence guns esp. its RPGs(Rocket Propelled Grenades) did the job. Also, a Ukrainian drone set ablaze a Russian fighter jet. And Russian troops were seen rummaging, looting and sifting through a Ukrainian grocery store in Kyiv. In response to a distress call sent out by Ukrainian President Vlodymyr Zelensky, Space X Supremo Elon Musk activated Space X's Starlink satellites over Ukraine bringing broadband services to broadband beleagured Ukraine. The Russian space agency ROSCOSMOS Chief General Dmitry Rogozin is furious with Mr.Musk for this. Further, on day 6 of fighting, Ukraine claimed Russia fired "Grad" missiles in Kyiv and satellite imagery showed a 65 mile long Russian military convoy, armored vehicles and trucks inching forward in Ukraine. In the face of Western inaction and withdrawl, the global weighscales may tilt in Russia's favor and Russia(and China) may emerge the new arbiters of the global balance of power altering the prevailing world order as obtaining at the end of World War II. This is indeed a grim prospect as both countries are not democracies and are at best authoritarian. America and the West need to act fast and act firm to preempt this.

As Russian rockets hit Kheron airport and Russian jets struck a shopping mall there, air raid sirens were heard throughout the night in Brovary. And heavy shelling on residential areas, more and more air raids, missile and drone strikes from both sides were common throughout Ukraine as a Russian jet struck at cars in Kharkiv, Ukraine's second largest city, killing hundreds in the blink of an eye. Ukrainians in Mariupol were seen blocking a Russian military convoy. Also, the steady refugee influx from Ukraine touched a peak 500,000 on day 6 of fighting. As Australian PM Scott John "Sco Mo" Morrison announced $70 million in lethal and non-lethal aid to Ukraine, Canada moved to impose an oil embargo on Russia which is likely to impact the Canadian economy. And in a sports embargo, FIFA and UEFA kicked Russia out of FIFA World Cup and

UEFA boycotted Russian atheletes.

Meanwhile as Washington moves to shut its Embassy in Minsk, Belarus and suspends its operations Belarus has voted to go nuclear on the side of Russia. More, Russian troops many of them in Ukrainian Army fatigues for camouflage have been entering Ukraine through Belarus and what's more Belarus troops have been spotted in Gomel, Ukraine and Ukrainian authorities have made it clear anybody without a pass will be presumed a Russian saboteur as they press all Ukrainian men aged 18-66 in the fight against Russia even as the Ukranian Territorial Reserve forces join the fight against Russia and its women and children head for the borders. And Ukrainian nationals in New Delhi held a candle light vigil in front of the Ukrainian Embassy in Delhi. Also Ukranians sang Ukraine's national anthem in front of the government building in Kyiv. Further, Ukrainian Reserve forces are receiving training in first aid and similar matters. And in heavy bombardment from the Ukrainian side in Bagus, Mariupol, Ukraine claimed to have killed 500 Russian troops in toto till date since the start of the war even as it released pictures of razed ruins of thousands of cars hit by Russian missiles in Bagus. And there seem to be European Union, Syrian, Libyan and other nationals still stuck in Ukraine even on day 101th of the war. Further, adding itself to the long list of nations taking stringent action against Russia, Japan removed Russia from the list of nations enjoying MFN status and adopted international sanctions against Russia. Taking a cue from America, India too should recall Indian diplomats in Minsk like Head of Chancery Bhavika Mangalanandan, Attache Keshav Kumar and scale down its diplomatic presence in Minsk in protest against Putin's move but India traditionally seems to find comfort in siding with Moscow. But, international equations are fast changing and in a very important development with international ramifications, China in a tactically timed message released at the end of the Russian-Ukrainian talks in Belarus (in which Ukraine said a total Russian troop pullout from Crimea and Donbass and a ceasefire was very much on the table, something which may not go down well with Moscow on day 5 of war), sided with Russia maintaining sanctions were not the answer to Putin's bellicosity and said trade with Moscow would continue.

There is an implicit message in this for New Delhi and the new found Sino-Russian bonhomie and camaradie is reminiscent of the 50s and 60s. Indeed, there are no permanent friends or enemies in politics and political friends make for strange bedfellows. So, India should shed its traditional disdain for the West, recognise the new altered geopolitical realities and come out in open defaince of the wily and crafty Putin who is playing a double game against India. This is not only organic, natural, scientific and logical but its in India's national interest and in tune with the principles of natural justice and in the fitness of things. Also, the new found Sino-Russian camaradie offers a glimpse into the behind the scenes goings on in the Sino-Russian dynamic in normal times. China also rued the eastward expansion of NATO. And still on NATO's expansion, Finnish President Sauli Vainamo Ninisto made it known Finland would join NATO and prior to this, Russian President Vladimir Putin made it clear his country would "punish" Finland by cutting off its power supplies if it joined NATO. And now obviously this is a certainty.And in the latest on this, the Kremlin issued a chilling warning to Finland saying "it could destroy Finland in 10 seconds".

And never mind the Russian warning, Sweden too seems to be following in the footsteps of Finland as Putin warned any amassing of troops on its borders would not be tolerated. And finally despite Russian threats, Sweden finally joined NATO on May 18, 2022. Welcoming them into the NATO fold, NATO Secretary General Jens Stoltenberg made it clear aggression of the sort that Russia showed in Ukraine would not be tolerated even as the Kremlin once again reiterated any amassing of troops on its borders would not be tolerated. And will Russia use tactical nuclear weapons in Ukraine? May be not or may be yes. History has been full of wars nobody thought would happen. On June 1, 2022, America finally woke up from its slumber and made it clear it would supply weapons to Ukraine, a move that Russia termed "unprecedented and dangerous" even as the Mayor of Kyiv said the enemy was closing in and was on the outskirts of the city.

But, beyond the headlines and between the lines the America-led NATO may not do much to challenge the Russian invasion of Ukraine as Ukraine is not a member of NATO. Ukraine for its part, continues to claim Crimea as part of its territory supported by a majority of governments led by the America-led West under UN Resolution 62/168 while some governments mostly the Russian leaning ones led by Russia recognise Crimea to be a part of Russia. Meanwhile, global crude prices led by the benchmark Brent crude acquired wings as they saw a sharp spike. Brent crude, for e.g., saw the highest spike since 2019. And taking the cue, other crudes like North Slope, the Indonesian Arjun etc. also registered an upward swing. 10% of all Russian oil, of which Russia is a major producer, passes through Ukraine but India sees no threat to its supplies as it grapples with the unfolding developments. As PM Modi chairs meeting after high level meeting on Ukraine and the External Affairs Ministry sets up a center for Indians stuck in Ukraine esp. students, Indian nationals have been left largely fending for themselves and this they are doing by routing their return to India through countries such as Rumania, Hungary and other East European countries and in this they say Indian Embassies in the region have been helpful.

And on Day 5 of fighting senior Indian Ministers are fanning out to Hungary, Poland and Slovakia as the PM's special envoys to oversee evacuation and rescue operations of Indians stuck in Ukraine and neighboring East European and Central European countries. While Civil Aviation, Urban Development, Housing, New and Non-Renewable Energy Minister and former UN Ambassador Hardeep Singh Puri is our point man in Hungary, Roads and Highways Minister Gen.(retd.) V.K.Singh will go to Poland while a third Minister Jyotiraditya Scindia will oversee rescue and relief operations in Slovakia even as Slovakia coming out on Ukraine's side made it clear it will send weapons supplies to war torn Ukraine including air defence missiles and anti-tank missiles as a steady refugee influx floods the Hungarian Slovak border. And, well, a full blown war is underway. And to the charge that India was fuelling Russia's Ukraine war by buying Russian oil, Foreign Minister Dr.Subramanyam Jaishankar, Dr.S.Jaishankar retorted by levelling the counter charge that Why was Venezuelan oil not allowed to come into the market? Why was Iranian oil not allowed to come into the market? Whatever, for all the powers concerned, India or otherwise, Russian oil is a marriage of convenience. And as an increasing number of Russian generals meet the kiss of death in Russia's Ukraine war, Putin has recalled one Gen.Pavel from retirement to lead the charge upfront. Whether this is first Russian Chief of Army Staff(COAS) and Adjuntant General Pavel Gavrilovich Gagarin or not is uncertain. Whatever, Russia seems to be headed for a long haul in Ukraine.

And showing it was Russia versus the world, traditionally neutral Switzerland joined the clarion call of increasing number of countries coming out in Ukraine's support as Ukraine grapples with the Russian bear. Newly elected Swiss President Ignazio Cassis, a former Foreign Minister, said Switzerland would adopt EU sanctions against Russia.

Indian Ambassador to Switzerland Monika Kapil Mohta, a former Ambassador to Sweden, Poland and Lithuania apart from serving senior diplomatic assignments in far flung corners of the world should get first hand information from the Swiss government on this interesting turn of events. Poland said it would send its fleet of Mig-29s to Ramstein Air Base, Germany and put them at the disposal of the United States for use in Ukraine. But, this is the proverbial over enthusiasm of new converts that brought Ukraine to peril. And slowly the America-led West is being galvanised into action. The American Senate released funds for use in Ukraine. European countries are mobilising their military helicopters. And, in a key development, Russian troops took charge of two Ukrainian nuclear power plants including the Chernobyl nuclear power plant. Spanish Foreign Minister Jose Manuel also signalled two planes loaded with humanitarian aid esp.medicines had landed in Kyiv. Importantly, there are limited food and water supplies may be to last a week although on the face of it the situation does appear rather rosy. But, this is not true. India, too, is sending humanitarian aid including medicines to Ukraine. As Russian-Ukrainian talks in Belarus appear inconclusive, China has stirred the mix by coming out in open support of Moscow's Ukraine policy. Also, as Putin readies nuclear plan which would be a catastrophe Russian troops seem to have bypassed Kharkiv, Ukraine's second largest city. The Russians also seized a Ukrainian missile launcher and Russian aircraft bombed Ukrainian missile depots, ports and the like. In related developments, Indonesia dumped its Su-35 deal with Russia as it contemplates going in for Western variants like the American F-16 or the French Rafale. CAASTA(Combatting America's Adversaries through Sanctions) effect? Perhaps. Still on CAASTA, America, despite CAASTA and similar laws, doesn't seem to be in a position to do anything about some of its adversaries, notably North Korea, which seems to engaging in carousel ICBM launching with a spree of ICBM launches, the latest one being a Gaum class ICBM capable of reaching the outer reaches of the Strastosphere far beyond. One last point on Ukraine(which is a hot developing story and we have to see how the conflict fans out. Will Kyiv fall or will the situation be resolved amicably through talks? The floor is open.) before I close the discussion on Ukraine for now is in personal punitive sanctions, America imposed personal punitive sanctions on Mr.Putin(for e.g. Mr.Putin cannot now fly abroad to the West as Germany becomes yet another country to close its air space to Russian planes), Russian Foreign Minister Sergei Victorovich Lavrov, Defence Minister Sergei Kuzhugetovich Shoigu, Chief of the General Staff Valery Valentinovich Gerasimov and other senior Russian officials. The latest on this is the

America-led West imposed punitive sanctions on Putin's two daughters. But, experts say these measures may not have much effect. Russia, for its part, dropped a bombshell. In what is the financial equivalent of dropping a nuclear bomb, Russia, pegged the Rouble to gold delivering a body blow to the $ and Western currencies. Worse, Russia said henceforth the West could buy Russian oil only against gold. Finally, on April 19, 2022, Russia's Ukraine War reached the 100th day and on the 100th Russia destroyed weapons that America had supplied to Ukraine. Also, Russia lashed out at the America-led West for supplying weapons to Ukraine and said World War III was a distinct possibility even as the White House called upon the international community to reduce the frequency of statements issued regarding nuclear war. Among other noteworthy developments is news that Iran may develop nuclear weapons in April-May 2022. Coming back to Ukraine, fierce fighting went on centered around Mariupol even as the Russians tried to secure a steel plant there. And the Ajog regiment which had until now defended the steel plant finally surrendered to the Russians on May 18, 2022 with the Russians making it known they would be charged with terrorism for which purpose legislation was brought forward in the Duma. The Ukrainians, for their part, are trying to secure rear lines and push back the Russians from key cities. And the latest on this is that Putin will likely resort to imposing martial law in Ukraine one Russia overrides Ukraine which is only a matter of time. Meanwhile, Starlink has 'destroyed' Putin's information campaign.

And the Indian Navy's 5th Scorpene class submarine, the Vagir, looks all set for maiden sea trials. India's Rafale multi-role fighter bombers have multi-fold and varied capabilities cutting across the spectrum. Also American media reports have it that India has placed an order for American F/A 18E Super Hornets for its carrier based fleet of aircraft. And in a comment on Indian foreign policy esp. its penchant for diversifying its defense resource base, Russian Mig-29K naval multi-role fighters service and take off the decks of India's Russian acquired aircraft carrier INS Vikramaditya(Admiral Gorshkov).

Still on American F/A 18Es, the USS Harry.S.Truman conducted maneouvres in formation with F/A 18E Super Hornets even as the USS Carl Vinson conducted joint survellance operations with Taiwanese naval units in the South China Sea in a move to flag China. And Canada placed an order with Boeing for P-8 joint patrol aircraft to replace its ageing C-40 aircraft as the US said it had no plans to buy additional P-8s from Boeing. Further, Leonardo's P-122 light utility helo has a top notch speed of 169.9 nautical miles per hour or 162.9 mph. While America's F-35B Lightning II is the most capable and deadly fighter to ever come out of the assembly jig, a fleet of F-22 Raptors, F-35s and Rafales will defend the UAE against the Houthis as the Houthis slammed a SAM and sent it hurtling into Abu Dhabi airport. And as of Feb. 2022, the United States is sending USAF B-52 strategic bombers to the United Kingdom as part of a Bomber Task Force and 4 have already arrived in Britain. Sitting ducks for S-350 missiles? Perhaps. Also, America's F-35s alongwith Russian and European fighter aircraft are among the top 5 fighter aircraft of the world while USS America is the world's most ambitious assault amphibious vessel LRA with no peer.

Solar geomagnetic storms have also downed 40-49 Space X Starlink satellites in a day in early Feb.2022. But the path of these storms and flares is quite predictable so it beats one how scientists could not have foreseen it. The possible reason could be these flares have a drag on the atmosphere which is unavoidable and which can knock out satellites. Also, Space X received authorization to offer broadband services from its satellites but when it placed a request with NASA for satellite deployment, NASA balked. Space rivalries? Good. It will keep space agencies on their toes. And scientists have zeroed in on 1000 galaxies in our cosmic neighbourhood alone and made the startling discovery that black holes could be at the center of galaxies even as they discover a rogue black hole i.e. a blackhole which has spun off its orbit. And Einstein's brilliance is dazzling. He predicted that 90 million years from now, two supermassive blackholes will collide with cataclysmic consequences. But, even the great Einstein couldn't/didn't think of the expanding universe as he put forward the Cosmological Constant. He was later proved wrong.

The Universe is indeed expanding and like spots on an expanding balloon, the galaxies are moving away from each other. But, what is the Universe expanding into. This, scientists are not sure. And remember, here we are talking of the ENTIRE Universe. Which is the largest galaxy? While most people think AC 1105 which spans 6 million light years, the truth is otherwise with the radiojets of Alcyoneus taking the cake spanning 16 million light years. Scientists have discovered a new planet in our solar system's vicinity, so, let's protect the planet before man does to it what he did to this planet. Further, oceans are getting darker because of pollution with plastic reaching even the Mariana Trench. Also, can consciousness exist in dual dimensions? Talking of dimensions, there are not two, not three, not four, not five but as many as twenty five different dimensions. And recently declassified videos released by a former Pentagon employee point to the existence of extraterrestrial life.

Moving on, in what may prove to be a race against time, America has to retrieve one its lost F-16C(an intelligence prize for the Chinese and the Russians which they can reverse engineer) aircraft that it lost in the South China sea before the Russians or the Chinese can lay their hands on it. Also, China has supplied truck borne Motorized Howitzers for arms parity with India. And it is ARAGA gun control systems for the Indian Army. Amidst the armed skirmishes between the Indian Army and the PLA, its Make in India drones for surveillance at the LAC. And the Typhoon class nuclear submarines are the largest undersea vessels ever built. Further, Russian weapons are at least a generation behind their Western counterparts but the Russian RPGs(Rocket Propelled Grenades) which are as ubiquitous and popular as ever are an exception. Recently, there was a "dogfight" between Mig-29s and Su-27s over Africa. As India supplies military defense command systems for Spanish JF-45 and JF-47 Chinook helos, Multi-role Maritime Mission Aircraft(MMMA)s have been supplied to the Indian Navy. Also, Britain has roped in Lockheed Martin for military supplies to its forces and Lockheed Martin has admitted it faces anti-trust roadblock. Continuing the discussion further, in a move to test Taiwan's defenses, China deployed its JF-16D Electronic Warfare jets at the contested Taiwan Straits and Taiwan moved F-14 Tomcat fighters on to its borders with China to test China's resolve. Three cheers for David! China has also tested a totally new kind of hypersonic technology as it breaks a new speed barrier and heralds a new kind of technology hetherto thought impossible. And as an increasing number of countries shut their door on *"pariah"*

China, Italy becomes the latest country to do so, kicking out a Chinese company that tried to sell drones to Italy. And cocking a snook at China haters, are Chinese investors, who seem to be saying "hate China?", "Will dump money in your country". And regarding Indian participation in the 2022 Beijing Winter Olympics, there are conflicting reports regarding the Indian participation. While some reports suggest India is one among 16 countries to boycott the Games, more reliable reports suggest an Indian contingent led by Sports Secretary Arif Khan is there very much in Beijing. And the Tejas Mk II has gone on the assembly jig as the Tejas LCA is unveiled at the Singapore Air show where it is expected to demonstrate its superior capabilities. Talking of Southeast Asian fighter capabilities, they range from Singapore's F-15s to Vietnam's Sukhoi-30s and Sukhoi-57s.Also in an embarrasing incident for America, Iran based Houthi rebels shot down a Royal Saudi Air Force F-15 with nothing more than old improvised anti-aircraft missiles. This writer made a mention of the other super weapons America has produced in one of this writer's other articles. At the risk of elucidation, the writer will mention them at the end of this book.

II

The American Military

The United States Armed Forces include the Army, Navy, Air force, the apex Chairman of the Joint Chiefs of Staff Committee who is the single point military adviser to the President, National Security Council and the Homeland Security Council, the civilian Secretary of the Air Force to whom the Chief of Air Staff acts as the military deputy, the Secretary of the Army to whom the Chief of Army Staff acts as the military deputy and the Secretary of the Navy to whom the Chief of Naval Operations acts as the military deputy, the U.S. Marines, NORAD(North American Air Defense Command), Strategic Air Command(Strat. Com), the Space Forces and the Marine Airlift Command.

The Navy

The Chief of Naval Operations

Let us start with the Navy as the United States is primarily a naval power (in the words of Harry. S. Truman "the Navy forms the bulwark of our defense forces as 3/4ths of the world is covered by water"). Unlike in India or even Pakistan, the U.S. Chief of Naval Operations does not exercise operational command over the Navy. That is left to the respective combatant commanders who report directly to the Secretary of Defense. However, as the designee of the Secretary of the Navy, he does exercise control over Navy units and organizations. In other words, the US has theatre commands which India is now contemplating being a brainchild of late CDS Gen.Bipin Rawat in India.

The very first U.S. Chief of Naval Staff was Admiral William. S. Benson who was followed by a succession of Navy Chiefs like Admiral Robert. R. Coontz, Admiral William Standley (the very first Chief of Naval Staff to become Chairman of Joint Chiefs of Staff Committee), Admiral William D. Leahy (Chairman, Joint Chiefs of Staff Committee, signed the London Naval Treaty in 1930 on behalf of the United States), Admiral Elmo M Zumwait (after whom the U.S. Zumwiat class destroyer is named), Admiral Harold. R. Stark, Admiral James Watkins (a former Secretary of Energy who was Commander in Chief of the U.S. and Allied Forces, Pacific Ocean Areas and Commander in Chief, U.S. Pacific Fleet), the five-star General, Admiral Chester. W. Nimitz (after whom the now decommissioned Vietnam-era Aircraft Carrier U.S.S. Nimitz which sometime back docked at Chennai dockyards is named), Admiral Charles. R. King, Admiral Forrest. P. Sherman, Admiral Michael. 'Mike' Muellen, a Chairman, Joint Chiefs of Staff Committee, Admiral Gary Roughhead(Commander in Chief of the U.S. Pacific Fleet, Surface Warfare Officer), Admiral Jonathan. W. Greenert(Submarine Officer), Admiral John M Richardson(Chief of Naval Staff, Director of U.S. Navy Nuclear Propulsion, Submarine Warfare Officer, Commands held U.S. Navy Naval Forces, Norfolk Submarine Group 8, U.S.S.Honolulu), and the present Chief of Naval Operations Admiral Michael. M. Gilday(Chief of Naval Staff, Surface Warfare Officer) and others.

The Indo-US Pacific Command

The United States Indo-US Pacific Command, formerly the U.S. Pacific Command with headquarters at Hawaii is America's oldest and largest of theatre commands. Its geographical spread includes wildlife from kolas to tigers. The present Commander-in-Chief of the U.S. Indo-US Pacific Command is Admiral Philip. S. Davidson U.S. Navy preceded by Admiral Harry Bailey Harris, Admiral Harry. B. Harris, now U.S. Ambassador to South Korea. The Commander-in-Chief of the U.S. Pacific Fleet is Admiral John. C. Aquilino, a former Commander being John Swinton. The Deputy Commander-in-Chief of the U.S. Indo-U.S. Pacific Command is Lt. General Bryan. P. Fontaine.

The U.S. Marines

The Commandant of U.S. Marine Corps is typically the highest-ranking uniformed officer in the U.S. Marine Corps and is a member of the Joint Chiefs of Staff and reports to the Secretary of the Navy directly and advises the President, Secretary of Defense, National Security Council, Homeland Security Council and the Secretary of the Navy on all matters pertaining to the U.S. Marine Corps and as such is responsible for all plans, policies, programs etc. pertaining to the U.S. Marine Corps and allocates resources etc. to the Unified Combatant Commands. Like the Chief of Army Staff, Chief of Air Staff, and the Chief of Naval Operations, being an administrative position, he does not exercise operational command over the U.S. Marine Corps. His seat is in the Pentagon, Arlington County, Virginia, and his residences are at Marine Barracks, Washington D.C. The present Commandant is Gen. David H. Berger, preceded by Gen. Robert Blake Neller, Robert. B. Neller, Gen Joseph Francis Joe. F. Dunford Jr., other Commandants include Gen. James. L. Jones, and the very first Commandant of the Continental Marines as the U.S. Marines were then known is Gen. Samuel Nicholson, among others.

The Chief of Air Staff

Like the Chief of Naval Operations, the Chief of Air Staff does not exercise operational command over the Air force, that is left to the combatant commanders who report directly to the Secretary of Defense. However, as the designee of the Secretary of the Air Force, he does exercise command over Air Force units and organizations. The precursor to the Chief of Air Staff was the Commanding

General of the Army Air Forces who led U.S. and Allied forces during World War II the first being Henry. H. Arnold.

The very first Air Chief was Air Force General Carl A. Spatz who was followed by a succession of Air Chiefs like Thomas. D. White, George. S. Brown, Nathan. F. Twining, all three of whom went on to become Chairmen, Joint Chiefs of Staff Committee, Hoyt. S. Vandenburg, Curtis. E. LeMay, Larry. D. Welch, John. M. Loh, Ronald. R. Fogleman, Michael. E. Ryan, John. P. Jumper, Air Force General Richard Bowman Myers, Air Force General Richard. B. Myers, a Chairman, Joint Chiefs of Staff Committee, John. D. Ryan, Charles. A. Gabriel, John. P. McDonnell who took office on 1st February,1965, Michael Dugan (who was born in 1931), Merrill. A. McPeak, Lew Allen. Jr, Ralph. E. Eberhart, T. Michael Mosely who was sacked along with then Secretary of the Air Force Michael Wynne after the accidental transportation of a nuclear weapon from Minot Air Force Base, North Dakota to Barksdale Air Force Base, Louisiana, and the shipment of some nuclear parts to Taiwan which while itself not dangerous, nevertheless irritated China, Duncan. J. McNabb, Norton. A. Schwartz, Mark. A. Welsh III, David. L. Goldfien who received his commission from the U.S. Air Force Academy in 1983 and who graduated from the U.S. Air Force Weapons School and is a command pilot with over 4,200 hours of flying experience flying T-37, T-38, F-16 C/D, MU- 37 and MT-72 aircraft and who flew a F-16 at Jodhpur Air Base on a visit to India some time back (2020), the incumbent and the first black to hold the job who took office on August 6th, 2020, Air Force General Charles. Q. Brown and others. The residences of the U.S. Air Chief are at Quarters 7, Fort Myer.

The Chief of Army Staff

Much like the Chief of Air Staff and the Chief of Naval Operations, the U.S. Chief of Army Staff does not exercise operational command over the Army, a role left to the combatant commanders who report directly to the Secretary of Defense and much like the U.S. Navy or Air Force, the U.S. Chief of Army Staff does exercise control over Army units and organizations as the designee of the Secretary of the Army. According to a very recent statistic (as of 2021), perhaps unreliable, the U.S. Army moved to the No.2 spot in the world in size in the world just behind the PLA of China, followed by the Russian Army, pushing the Indian Army, until now the 2nd largest, to the 4th spot, followed by the Democratic Republic of Korea (North Korea) Army. According to the same statistic, The United States Armed Forces now occupy the No.1 spot in the world in terms of modernity of equipment, followed by the PLA Armed Forces of China. While the modernity of equipment part seems believable, since the statistic in question is controversial, as China moves to make its forces leaner and meaner, the global pecking order of armed forces in terms of manpower strength perhaps still remains the same i. e. PLA occupying the No.1 spot, followed by the Indian Army, with the United States Armed Forces coming up 3rd, followed by the Russian Army, followed by the Democratic Republic of Korea Army. Everything is an open question as these statistics keep fluctuating. Interestingly, Pakistan as part of its larger India paranoia, maintains armed forces far beyond its requirements, the 11th largest in size in the world.

The very first U.S. Chief of Army Staff was Lt. Gen. LTG Samuel. B. M. Young, followed by Gen. Adna Chaffee, followed Lt. Gen John. C. Bates, followed by Major General J. Franklin Bell. Other Army Chiefs include Gen. Malin Craig, Gen. Edward. C. Meyer, Gen. Eric. K. Shinseki, Gen. Maxwell. D. Taylor, Gen Ronald. K. Johnson, Gen. Omar Bradley, Gen. J. Lawton Collins, Gen. Matthew. B. Ridgeway, Gen. Maxwell. D. Taylor. Gen. Douglas. McArthur, Gen. George. C. Marshall, Gen. Dwight. D. Eisenhower, Gen. Lyman. L. Lemnitger, Gen. Earl. C. Wheeler, Gen. Bernard. W. Rogers, Gen. Mark Alexander Milley, Gen. Mark. A. Milley, now Chairman, Joint Chiefs of Staff Committee who contracted Covid-19 at the height of the Covid-19 pandemic, but later tested negative, the present Chief of Army Staff Gen James. C. McConville and many, many others.

The Chairman, Joint Chiefs of Staff Committee

As noted earlier the Chairman, Joint Chiefs of Staff Committee is the single point military advisor to the President, and apart from the President, reports to the Homeland Security Council and the National Security Council.

The very first Chairman, Joint Chiefs of Staff Committee was Gen. Earl. C. Wheeler followed by a long succession of Chairmen, Joint Chiefs of Staff Committee that includes former Secretary of State (during the Reagan era), the handsome Gen. Alexander. M. Haig, Gen. Colin. L. Powell, Air Force General Richard Bowman Myers Air Force General Richard. B. Myers, Admiral Michael. 'Mike.' Muellen, Air Force Gen Nathan. F. Twining, Thomas. D. White, George. S. Brown, Admiral William Standley, Admiral William. D. Leahy, Admiral Chester. W. Nimitz, Air Force Gen Peter Pace, Gen. Lyman. L. Lemnitzer, Joseph

Francis Joe. F. Dunford Jr. and the present Gen. Mark Alexander Milley, Mark. A. Milley.

Deputy Chairman, Joint Chiefs of Staff Committee include Air Force General Paul. J. Selva and the present Gen. John Earl Hyten, John. E. Hyten, a former Strategic Air Command, Strat. Com Commander.

Secretary of the Air Force

The Secretary of the Air Force, the civilian deputy to the Secretary of Defense, is the Chief Executive of the Department of Air Force, and his salary as with the Secretary of the Army or the Secretary of the Navy is as per Executive Schedule Level II.

Apart from others, Secretaries of the Air Force include the very first Stuart Symington followed by Thomas. K. Finletter, David. C. Young, Robert. E. Seaman, Hans Mark, Thomas Young, Heather Ann Wilson, Michael Wynne, Barbara Barrett, Acting Secretary of the Air Force John. P. Roth and the incumbent Frank Kendall who is a distinguished graduate of the military academy at West Point.

Secretary of the Army

The Secretary of the Army, the civilian deputy to the Secretary of Defense is the chief executive of the Department of Army.

Among others, Secretaries of the Army include the very first Kenneth Claiborne Royall, former Deputy Secretary of State (during the Jimmy Carter era) Cyrus Vance, former Defense Secretary Mark Thomas Esper who served in the U.S. 102nd Air Borne Division during the Gulf War, Ryan Mc

Carthy, Acting Secretary of the Army John. E. Whitley, John. M. Mc Hugh who served 2010-2013, and the incumbent Christine Wormuth, who became the first woman Secretary of the Army.

Secretary of the Navy

The Secretary of the Navy, the civilian Deputy to the Secretary of Defense is the chief executive of the Department of Navy.

The very first Secretary of the Navy was Benjamin Stoddart, followed by 77 Secretaries of the Navy. Among others, some of them are first Secretary of Defense James Vincent Forrestal, James. V. Forrestal, second American President John Adams who also served as first United States Ambassador to Netherlands besides serving as first American Secretary of State, Francis William Mathews, Benjamin Franklin, James Edwin McPherson, James. E. McPherson, Ray Maybus, Thomas Modly, Richard Vaughn Spencer, former Ambassador to Norway, former town councilman and businessman Kenneth John Braithwaithe who served in the U.S. Navy Reserve, and the present Acting Secretary of the Navy Thomas. W. Harker who had to put in his papers following a snowballing "controversial comments on Covid-19 scandal" which cost him his job. However, Mr. Harker as of late May 2021 continues as the Acting Secretary of the Navy pending the appointment of a permanent Secretary of the Navy.

NORAD (North American Aerospace Defense Command) Commander

The Commander of NORAD set up to pre-empt and thwart a possible Russian or Chinese nuclear attack from the North Pole or Arctic, until 2001 the Commander-in-Chief of NORAD is the head of all US and Canadian operational military command forces on North American territory and concurrently serves as the Commander of the United States Northern Command. The headquarters of NORAD are in Cheyenne Mountain Complex, El Paso County, Ohio.

NORAD Commanders

The very first Commander of NORAD was Gen. Earl. E. Partridge followed by a succession of Commanders that include Gen. Raymond. J. Reeves, Gen. Seth. J. Mckee, Gen. Dennis James Jr., Gen. James. E. Hill, Air Force General Richard Bowman Myers Richard. B. Myers, Gen. Timothy. J. Keating, Air Force General Ralph. E. Eberhardt Air Force General Terrence John O Shaughnessy, Terrence. J. O. Shaughnessy and the present Gen. Glen. D. VanHerck and others.

Strategic Air Command (Strat. Com) Commander-in-Chief

America's Strategic Air Command is the body that oversees America's strategic nuclear triad comprising of 450 land-based ICBMs (deep into the countryside of Maryland for e.g., hundreds of ICBMs take off from silos on the orders of the President of the United States in case of nuclear war), nuclear submarines buried under the oceans of the world and air borne bombers.

The present Commander-in-Chief of Strat.Com reporting directly to the President of United States and the Secretary of Defense is Admiral Charles. A. Richard preceded by Gen. John Earl Hyten, John. E. Hyten among others.

Space Forces Commanders

The present Commander of the United States Space Forces (the United States is just among two countries in the world with its own Space Forces, the other being Russia. In fact, the United States was the first country in the world to add a Space Forces Component to its arsenal) responsible for aerospace warfare is Gen. John. W. J. Raymond preceded by Steve Kwast, preceded by Air Force General Richard Bowman Myers, Richard. B. Myers and others.

Supreme Allied Commander Europe (SACEUR)

The Supreme Allied Commander Europe (SACEUR) reporting directly to the NATO Secretary General, currently Jens Stoltenberg, via the NATO Military Committee with headquarters at Mons, Casteu, Belgium is the head of all U.S. and Allied Forces in Europe. The position has always been held by a U.S. General currently Air Force General Todd. D. Walters, preceded by Gen. (now Senator) Curtis. M. Scaparotti, Bernard. W. Rogers, John Galvin, Wesley Clark Jr., Gen. John Shalikashvili, General Alexander. M. Haig, General Lyman. L. Lemnitzer, Air Force General (French Air Force) Dennis Mitchell, Lord Earl Mountbatten and others.

The US Department of Defense

The US Department of Defense is led by the Secretary of Defense who is assisted by the Assistant Secretaries of Defense who in turn are assisted by the Under Secretaries of Defense. The apex level senior officials lead officials like the Inspector General and agencies like the Defense Intelligence Agency and other agencies. Then further down the pyramid are various commands like the Strategic Air Command, Aerospace Defense Command, and the Marine

Airlift Command. At the base of the pyramid are the geographic commands like the Pacific Command, the Atlantic Command, the European Command, the Central Command the African Command, the Southern Command, and the Northern Command.

Among nuclear weapon states, designated nuclear weapon states are the United States, Russia, the UK, France, and China. States known to possess nuclear weapons are India, Pakistan, and North Korea. States thought to possess nuclear weapons are Israel. NATO member countries hosting nuclear weapons are Belgium, Germany, the Netherlands, and Italy. States formerly possessing nuclear weapons are Ukraine, Belarus, Kazakhstan and South Africa and the candidate countries are well known, they are Canada, Australia, Germany, Japan, Iran (could even be actively pursuing a nuclear weapons program, despite a Nuclear Deal with the West which was later called off by Iran. Iran even claims to have developed a nuclear engine and might be working on Uranium enrichment) etc.

Some years back, an American drone, the RQ-179 Sentinel, crashed in Qom, Iran and speculation was rife in American and Western circles that the next day's flights from Moscow and Beijing would be full, with the Russians and the Chinese trying to reverse engineer the drone as in modern warfare drones are an esp. effective way of combat as they can be used to hover over an area for hours together mapping military sites and the like.

III

Other American Weapons

Other weapons in the American stockpile include the fastest fighter plane on Earth, the F-18A/E Super Hornet, the F-22 Raptor and the F-117A. Famous as the fastest plane ever built the F-117A was the result of early Russian indiscretions on radar technology. The aircraft is less known for its stealth features. It is also equipped with fly by wire technologies which prevent the aircraft from spinning out of control while in flight. The F-22 Raptor, which is the latest from the American inventory, has already joined service. Then there is the S-71 whose efficacy was proved in Operation Odyssey Dawn in Libya. Coming to the B-2 Spirit Stealth Bomber, former American Defense Secretary Gen James 'Mad Dog' Jim Mattis testifying before the Senate disclosed that out of the total 72 B-2 Stealth Bombers in operation 18 were the maintenance depot and out of the remaining, only 36 were in active service as of 2018. The B-2 uses a technology which cuts of all energy emissions and thereby evades detection. This in other words is stealth technology. The B-2 was designed to penetrate Soviet air defenses at night during war time. It was used during Operation Desert Storm in Iraq to enforce no fly zones. America used lot of draconian measures during the Iraq War like using bombs which suck out oxygen from the lungs which brings back memories of Napalm bombs used during the Vietnam war before the Silent Majority [acting in response to the steady inflow of body bags (dead American soldiers) put paid to Nixon's plans to secure an outright military victory over Vietnam]. Coming back to the Iraq War, not to be outdone, Saddam Hussein, with whom India's Foreign Minister Bali Ram Bhagat, a former Speaker of the Lok Sabha, did a tete e tete, stole 4000 pages of laser enrichment of Uranium to put them to equally devious means. As regards Uranium enrichment, it refers to the process where Uranium gas is passed through centrifuges as part of a larger plan which includes possible building of atom bombs.

American Space and Nuclear Facilities

American Space Facilities include Cape Canaveral or Cape Kennedy, Houston, Texas and of course NASA. On the topic of NASA, NASA 2020 announced the Artemis Program (sister of Apollo, Greek Goddess of Moon) to place the first woman, the next man and the first person of color on the Moon by 2025 and establish a sustainable human lunar presence by the end of the decade. For this purpose, it has shortlisted a clutch of 21 astronauts of which only three will finally go to the Moon, at least one of whom will be a woman. The shortlist is as follows-Raja Chari who was born in Milwaukee, Wisconsin, Jessica Watkins, Matthew

Dominic, Kyla Barron, Johnny Kim, Francisco Rubio, Robert Hines, Loral O'Hara, Zana Cardman, Canadians Joshua Kutryk, Jenny Sidey Gibbons, Jeremy Hansen and Charles Duboczhe, Joseph Acaba, Victor Glover, Kjell Lindgren, Anne McCain, Kate Rubins, Christina Hammock Knock, Jessica Meir and finally Stephanie Wilson. Of these Raja Chari is a F-16 fighter pilot with the U.S.Air Force while Zana Cardman who went to Harverd is a geobotanist and Kate Rubins harvested fresh Radishes off the Advanced Planet Habitat on board the International Space Station (ISS which, incidentally, is the fastest man-made object till date orbiting the Earth at a speed of 1,7,50,000 miles per min and which will crash come 2031 with India being one of the places where it may crash). Other possible landing sites include the Pacific etc), opening up further possibilities for space exploration and long duration missions to the Moon and Mars. And NASA hopes to use the Artemis pool of astronauts to first colonize the Moon and nearby areas and then polevault from thereon to Mars. But the Artemis mission which has run into time overruns seems to be jinxed from the start. The latest on this is that Artemis's I's asteroid probe has lost ground contact. The landmark Artemis mission may even become a still born.

Meanwhile, Space X's Elon Musk has said Space X will place a man on Mars by 2029 but many feel impulsive Mr.Musk has in the past had time overruns and failed to meet deadlines and this time too has acted in haste by announcing a deadline which is unrealistic and that he cannot meet. A more realistic deadline would be NASA's deadline of mid-2030s. But, as former NASA Administrator James "Jim" Bridenstine(present Administrators Steve Jurcyk and Bill Nelson) says "The first person on Mars is probably too young as yet". And for the Artemis II mission which as we noted earlier aims to place the first woman, the next man and the first person of color on the Moon, NASA has identified 13 possible landing sites and all are within 6 degrees of the latitude of Moon's South Pole which is of scientific significance as these are permanently shadowed areas full of natural resources and are as yet unexplored.

The latest on the Artemis mission is that NASA in a crucial change to its human space flight architecture is toying with the idea of adding a crew of astronauats to the current developmental flight of the Artemis mission currently under development and making Artemis II which will be launched in 2025 the final crewed mission. Also, Artemis I's Orion capsule sent to the Moon has already returned with a rich body of scientific literature and precious natural resources.

It was President Kennedy who first announced at Rice University that America would place a man on the Moon. It is worth noting that till now only 12 people have stepped on to the surface of the Moon, all men and all between 1969 and 1972. They are as follows: Neil Armstrong, Alwyn "Buzz" Edrin (Apollo 11), Charles "Pete" Conrad, Alan Bean (Apollo 12), no Apollo 13, Alan.B.Sheperd Jr., Edgar,D,Mitchell, David.R.Scott(Apollo 15), James.B.Irwin, John.W.Young (Apollo 14), Charles Duke (Apollo 16), Eugene "Gene" Cernan, and Harrison.H. Schmidt (Apollo 17). Of these only Alwyn "Buzz" Edrin, David Scott, Charles Duke and Harrison Schmidt are alive and Alwynn "Buzz" Edrin admitted he could not keep up with fame as he now suffers from Depression. The most recent to pass away was Alan Bean who passed away December 2020.

As is well known the first man in space was the Russian Dr. Yuri Alexei Gagarin and the second man and the first

American to orbit the Earth was Alan Shepard who went into space exactly 23 days after Gagarin on May 5th ,1961. The first woman in space was Valentina Tereshkova who into space in 1963 and first American woman in space was Sally Kirsten Ride who went into space in 1983. Sally Kirsten Ride went on to create history by becoming the first American woman fighter pilot in 1993.

On the topic of pilots, with regard to who is the youngest pilot in aviation history, there is a tie between Matt Guthmiller who circumnavigated the Earth, solo at the young age of 19 years, 7 months, 15 days and Anny Divya of India. Matt Guthmiller was educated at the Massachusetts Institute of Technology (MIT) and Anny Divya, a product of the Indira Gandhi Rashtriya Uran Academy became a commercial airline pilot at the young age of 19. Employed in Air India, Anny Divya, now 37, is now a Captain. Then there is Capt. Durga Banerjee who is on the top of the table in the world as regards women who have clocked up the maximum number of flying hours of experience, clocking up a whopping 18,500 flying hours of experience. However, unconfirmed reports have it that Jessica Levitt of the United States takes the cake among young pilots of the world becoming a pilot at, hold your breath, 9! However, the veracity of these reports is in question. Other young pilots include Kate McWilliams who at 26, became one of the youngest commercial airline pilots. Then there is Chinyere Kalu of Nigeria who is Nigeria's youngest commercial airline pilot. Kalu taught at the Nigerian Institute of Aviation Technology from Feb. 2011 to October 2014. The first African American fighter pilot was Jacques Bullard Johnson. The first pilot to fly solo across the Atlantic was of course Charles Lindbergh in 1931 and the first woman to do so was Amelia D' Hartley who did so in 1932. The STS-32 was launched on Feb.3, 1984, and on Feb.7th Bruce McCandless became the first person to float in space untethered by a chord when he stepped out of the space shuttle Challenger into nothingness. However, several years before that Alexei Leonov of Russia became the first person to float in space tethered by a 16-meter chord. Katherine Kathy Dwyer Sullivan is the first woman to float in space and she is also the first woman to dive to the 11-mile-deep Mariana Trench. James Cameron was the first man to dive to the Mariana Trench.

Two Japanese men laid claim to being the first Japanese man in space when they went into space at about the same time in September 1997. They are Koichi Wakata, an engineer and a veteran of the STS-57, STS-75, STS-117, STS-119 and STS-149 missions and Mohri Mamoru. The first Japanese woman to go into space was Dr. Mukai Chiaki, an engineer, and a physician. The first 7 of the 11 Chinese taikonauts (as Chinese astronauts are called 'taiko' meaning sky or space in Chinese) so far are Col. Yang Liwei (who went as part of the Shenzhou V capsule with Shenzhou VI being an acid test of China's tracking network which included tracking stations as far away as Namibia and four tracking ships placed around the oceans of the world), Nie Haisheng, Fei Junlong, Jing Haipheng, Liu Wang, Liu Yang , Wang Yapang and others. Of these Liu Yang and Wang Yapang are women. In this connection as noted by this author in one of his earlier writings, China has stolen a march over India in the race to Mars sending its solar powered Tianwen-I probe to Mars after Mangalyaan.

Tiawen-1 which carries an orbiter, lander and rover landed at Mars's North Pole and is carrying out excavations looking for water, ice, and other signs of life even as it sent spectacular close-up views of Mars. The latest on this front is that China has sent its newest and latest space station aboard a LM-3F rocket, the Tiangyong-3 June 2021 with taikonauts on board. Even minor powers like the UAE have sent probes to Mars after Mangalyaan like UAE's Al-Aqsa (Hope Peace) probe. Al-Aqsa will probe the Martian craters and look for other signs of life on Mars. Among moon probes apart from India's Chandrayaan-I and the failed Chandrayaan-II (it landed upside down due to a last-minute technical glitch. However, startling facts have emerged from the data sent by Chandrayaan about the Earth's only natural satellite, that there is water on the Moon and not small quantities but sufficient quantities ranging from two ounces per ton to 6 ounces per ton.) missions, China has sent the Chang E-4 to the dark side of the moon which in its efforts at sustaining a human lunar presence succeeded in growing a small seed of a potato plant on the moon. Also, NASA recently succeeded in hovering a helicopter over Mars. Here it is worth noting that due to the lack of atmosphere on Mars while on Earth a helicopter's rotor must carry out 120 rpm (revolutions per minute), in the rarified atmosphere of Mars it has to carry out 2,400 rpm.

NASA has also sent its New Horizons I and II spacecraft into the outer reaches of the solar system beyond Pluto and NASA's now dead Voyager and II spacecraft are the only man- made objects to have ever reached into interstellar space. They became dead recently after NASA gave two firings to their thrusters to prolong their life by 2 to 3 years. After further firings they are now active. Also, in the search for extra-terrestrial life, in 1978 in what came to be known as the 'Wow' signal at a NASA laboratory in Delaware, United States a strong radio frequency signal was felt for several seconds video graphic evidence of which is available. Extra-terrestrial life trying to contact us? Possibly. One never knows. Other efforts at tracing extraterrestrial life include the one in Cambridge, Lancashire, England at a former British nuclear testing site and of course the famous Hubble Space Telescope in Chile apart from numerous other facilities spread across the globe. Then there are of course the UFO sightings. In the realm of poetic speculation on extra-terrestrial are the strange statues on Easter Island, French Polynesia.

But, the James Webb(named after a former NASA Administrator, James.C.Webb) Space Telescope(JWST) launched on December 25, 2021 could rewrite Science and Astronomy books and offer a treat for Science and Astronomy buffs as it unlocks the truth about extraterrestrial life and peers under the atmosphere of exoplanets. It could prove to be the Holy Grail of Science, Astronomy and Astrophysics as it unlocks dark secrets about dark matter and dark energy. Unlike the Hubble which orbits the Earth, the JWST will orbit the Sun at the L1(Lagrange point named after a 18th Century mathematician, James Louis Lagrange who uncovered the truth behind the "three body theory" or why three bodies in a straight line don't change their relative positions) point. So far four Space Telescopes, Hubble, Spitzer, Chandra etc have been launched and none of them have been able to dig out the truth about extraterrestrial life and the JWST is expected to do exactly that operating in the infrared spectrum as it does unlike the Hubble and other space telescopes which operate in the X-Ray and visible light spectrum.

The JWST is also expected to unlock the truth behind our origins as it peers into the Universe 13.5 billion years ago soon after the Big Bang. And scientists say a previous cosmos, universe existed before the present one and the cosmic cycle will be repeated umpteen times. Also relativistic jets orbit binary star systems. Scientists have also found something "unlike any other seen before" in our Milky Way and the Andromeda are set to collide several billion years from now to form the Milkomeda. Binary star systems also give birth to second generation planets as planets form around dying stars. Incidentally, the Wilkinson Microwave Anisotrophy Probe fixed the age of the Universe at 13.5 billion years. And, finally, the JWST reached its final destination, the L1 point on Jan 26, 2022, a million miles from Earth. And as the JWST zeroes in its cameras on one of its first images, a star formation, it is increasingly becoming evident what the first images may be like and they are startling. The JWST is expected to unlock many, many, many other secrets of our Universe.

All this flies in the face of this starling piece of information-How far has human space exploration gone? Purportedly, according to scientists, one of the furthest regions that human spacecraft have gone lies beyond Pluto far beyond the Kuiper Belt, the 485956 Arrokoth, 27 billion km away from us. Before its official name was announced, the Arrokoth was known as the Ultima Thule or Snowman[the Ultima Thule has come to denote the unknown(to the English, this is Orkney Islands, off the Scottish Coast)]. Is Ultima Thule a planet? Scientists say Ultima Thule is just 22km in breadth and according to them it is a strange world of ice and rock consisting of strange phenomena like the Oort Cloud and strange areas like Huamea and Meamea. Here, scientists have encountered alien spacecraft and extraterrestrial beings. This bit is heresy while the other pieces of information may not be way off the mark. As scientists put it "we have never seen anything so primordial, so unchanged". And, according to them, it takes just 0.01gm of anti-matter to reach the Oort Cloud. However, human spacecraft, as earlier seen, HAVE gone far, far beyond 485956 Arrokoth right into the outer reaches of interstellar space(the Arrokoth was just part of the New Horizons Pluto flypast) like in the case(as noted earlier) of the Voyager I and II(stand corrected) spacecraft which as of 2018 received two to five firings extending their life by 5 years.

Further, in new Science, ever heard of a White Hole? Scientists believe the Big Bang that created the Universe was a White Hole implying that the source of all creation is a White Hole. Also, they have discovered a ninth planet, Nibiru, and they suspect the existence of a hypothetical tenth, Fatty. According to new Science, the Solar System doesn't end with Pluto but extends millions and millions of kilometers beyond the Kuiper Belt.

The Universe is truly puzzling. Phenomena like Tabby's Star and Diamond Star defy logic. For e.g., why does Diamond Star dim? No answer. And there are no answers to many things in the Universe. At least, not yet. Also, gas giant Jupiter is bigger than the rest of the planets of the solar system put together and it could "eat up", suck, the rest of the planets of the Solar System. Because it is made up of gas, Jupiter has retained most of its gas over the eons. Billions of years from now, Earth will cease to exist and some of the outer planets of the Solar System will probably exist but will move further away. And scientists believe Uranus's "wobble" is the result of a probable hit by a heavenly body, perhaps a meteor or a asteroid in the ancient past. And a crewed mission to Mars is likely to occur sooner than is popularly believed with Europe's mega rocket beating Space X at its own game. And Space X Starlink rocket could prove to be the Holy Grail of rocketry as it sets new standards for future rockets. Then, there is the revolutionary spacecraft that can take off from a runway and fly into space! And a new theory hints at what may lie beyond beyond the event horizon of a black hole and it is distant galaxies as seen through warmholes and also scientists believe one can see the end of the Universe at the other end of black holes and they also believe there are about 40 billion black holes in our galaxy alone.

And meet Blanets, planets orbiting black holes. Also, have humans stumbled upon a warp bubble? We may have. And there are also stunning images of a supernova explosion. Further, in a landmark development, the fastest man made object, the ISS which like an old car suffers from depreciation is at the fag end of its life and it will be retired in 2031 falling into the Pacific. But, ROSCOSMOS chief General Dmitry Rogozin said Feb.2022 the ISS is likely to fall in Russia, the EU or even India. Scientists also have detected a wierd signal coming from a cosmic source and it is in our neighbourhood. They have also solved the mystery of a pulsating radio signal coming from a cosmic source that has long puzzled scientists. Science holds that some black holes may be collapsed Universes. And like here on Earth, the Universe seems to love spirals and Science suggests that black holes and galaxies have spiral arms made of filaments of gas and dust, like the G 87 bone filament. In M 87 galaxy scientists have captured stunning images of a supernova explosion. Then, there is a new ASW rocket.

Also the Deep Space IA spacecraft launched in 1999 is the first spacecraft of its class to use ion engines instead of conventional rocket fuel and an ion engine spacecraft throws out ions from its afterburners at 1,44,000 times the speed of a conventional rocket. And scientists say, a surprising number of Exoplanets[which the Universe(or Universes?) is teeming with] may support alien life. And indeed they have found an Exoplanet that they feel is more suitable for life than Earth. And they have also found evidence of microbial life on Mars, C-12 carbon signatures(the basic ingradient for life) and water in Mars's Grand Canyon even as a Chinese lunar mission has found evidence of water on the Moon not to speak of India's very own Chandrayaan I mission which too found water on the Moon and not just in small quantities but large quantities. And here on Earth, scientists believe, the Earth's core(which according to a new theory houses a tropical forest full of possibilities of life) which is getting more and more lopsided may not be solid as was thougt of until now but instead may comprise of liquid ligaments and the like. And scientists have always believed Jupiter's largest moon Europa is a rich source of water under its ice caps. And Saturn's largest moon, Titan has a fascinating and stunning environment which has always fascinated scientists and now scientists believe it probably houses life. Still on Saturn, scientists have zeroed in on Saturn's Aurora, the strong electric winds whirling past at its North Pole as the possible reason for Saturn's strange magnetic field which has long baffled scientists.

Talking of extraterrestrial life, a Havard astronomer has suggested it may be nearer than we think. And some of the more laughable theories have it that the Universe may be teeming with "humans". And, among other things a Space X rocket is set to collide with the Moon 2022, a year which may see 42 space missions compared to 2021's 31 with an increasing use of Resusable Orbiters(RUOs). And, why is so much on Space and Science being discussed in a book on **World Military Order**? Because, many of these technologies are dual use technologies with military applications.

Continuing the the discussion, with regard to who is the youngest pilot in aviation history, there is a tie between Matt Guthmiller who circumnavigated the Earth, solo at the young age of 19 years, 7 months, 15 days and Anny Divya of India. Matt Guthmiller was educated at the Massachusetts Institute of Technology (MIT) and Anny Divya, a product of the Indira Gandhi Rashtriya Uran Academy became a commercial airline pilot at the young age of 19. Employed in Air India, Anny Divya, now 37, is now a Captain. Then there is Capt. Durga Banerjee who is on the top of the table in the world as regards women who have clocked up the maximum number of flying hours of experience, clocking up a whopping 18,500 flying hours of experience.

However, unconfirmed reports have it that Jessica Levitt of the United States takes the cake among young pilots of the world becoming a pilot at, hold your breath, 9! However, the veracity of these reports is in question. Other young pilots include Kate McWilliams who at 26, became one of the youngest commercial airline pilots. Then there is Chinyere Kalu of Nigeria who is Nigeria's youngest commercial airline pilot. Kalu taught at the Nigerian Institute of Aviation Technology from Feb. 2011 to October 2014. The first African American fighter pilot was Jacques Bullard Johnson. The first pilot to fly solo across the Atlantic was of course Charles Lindbergh in 1931 and the first woman to do so was Amelia D' Hartley which she did so in 1932. The STS-32 was launched on Feb.3, 1984, and on Feb.7th Bruce McCandless became the first person to float in space untethered by a chord when he stepped out of the space shuttle Challenger into nothingness. However, several years before that Alexei Leonov of Russia became the first person to float in space tethered by a 16-meter chord. Katherine Kathy Dwyer Sullivan is the first woman to float in space and she is also the first woman to dive to the 11-mile-deep Mariana Trench. James Cameron was the first man to dive to the Mariana Trench.

Continuing the topic of manned space missions, Lt. Guino Stewart Bufor Jr., a U.S. Air Force fighter pilot became the first black man in space when he went into space aboard the Challenger space shuttle while Mae Carol Jemison, an engineer and NASA astronaut, became the first black woman in space when she went into space aboard the Discovery space shuttle and Arnaldo Tamayo Mendez, a Cuban Air Force fighter pilot who was born in Guantanamo, Cuba became the first person of African descent to go into space when he did so as part of Russia's Soyuz mission. Prince Sheik Sultan Salman Abdul Aziz Al Saud, a Saudi Royal Air Force F-16 fighter pilot, became the first Arab, first Saudi citizen, first Muslim and only member of a royal family till date to go into space when he went as part of America's STS-57 mission. Anouseh Ansari was the first Arab woman in space while Hazza Al-Mansouri who went to the ISS along with NASA's Jessica Meir and Russia's Oleg Sripochka is the first Emirati to go into space. As is well known Desmond Tito (who had to cough up, shell out a whopping $1 million for his ride) is the world's only space tourist while Ashok Chakra Awardee Squadron Leader Rakesh Sharma who hopped on to Russia's Soyuz vehicle is the first Indian in space. Kalpana Chawla of Karnal was the first Indian woman in space when she went aboard an American vehicle. She, however, died in the Columbia space shuttle disaster. Possible causes of the disaster include an explosion of the shuttle's fuels and oxidizers, a navigational error which subtly changed the Columbia's angle of descent, or less likely a meteor strike or even less likely a terrorist sabotage. Whatever, the Columbia had fired its braking rockets and was about to land when it exploded in a ball of flame. Perhaps the Columbia could not withstand the extreme heats of re-entry. As the then American President Ronald Reagan noted Kalpana Chawla travelled the farthest into space. As is well known, preparations are afoot to launch the first Indian into space (called Gaganauts) aboard an indigenous brute of a Bahubali rocket. They are currently undergoing training at the Gagarin Flight School, Moscow and have already undergone training in high gravity acceleration near Bangalore including a test through an escape module. As part of this mission three Indians will go into space. It might be noteworthy that India is even constructing an astrodome or astronaut training center near Bangalore for future missions.

Frank Boreman, James.A.Lovell and William Anders are the first men to orbit the moon while William Shepherd, Yuri Gidzenko and James.A.Lovell are the first crew of the ISS. Vladimir Komarov was the first person to die in space while Japanese capsule Hayabushi was the first spacecraft to return with samples from an asteroid and Pioneer 9 and 10 were the first spacecraft to fly by Jupiter. The Cessna Huygens was the first spaceraft to fly by Saturn and its Cessna Hugyens 4 lander was the first orbiter to plunge into the atmosphere of Saturn and its last command was to study the aerodynamics of the spacecraft. The Mariner I was the first spacecraft to reach Mercury and the Mars

Orbiter was the first spacecraft to land on Mars. The Viking I and II spacecraft were the first spacecraft to reach Venus.

Earth falls within what is known as the Goldilocks Zone i.e. just the right distance from the Sun for water to exist in liquid form. Had it been any closer, the water would have evaporated and had it been any further away the water would have frozen. Indeed, such perfect symmetry exists in the Solar System itself what to speak of the Universe!. The largest volacano in the Solar System exists on Mars, the Olympus Mons volcano which is 21.8 km tall and the oldest known meteor is the Allende meteor which fell in Mexico in 1969 and which is 2.9 billion years old.

As for eclipses, a Solar Eclipse occurs when the moon comes in between the Earth and the Sun casting a shadow on Earth and a lunar eclipse occurs when the Earth, Moon and Sun are aligned together.

Returning to the topic of American Space and Nuclear facilities, apart from Cape Canaveral American Space and Nuclear facilities include the Los Almos Scientific Laboratories, California, the Jet Propulsion Laboratories, Pasadena, California, Smithsonian Institution, and many, many other lesser-known institutions. Of late private bodies like the Elon Musk headed Space X (or Space Xploration) which launched the world's first reusable rocket, the Halsen-9 and the world's first pair of electric satellites in collaboration with a French and an Asian consortium and the Richard Branson headed Virgin Galactic which launched the world's first Space Plane which travels at 3 imes the speed of sound or Mach 3 and has a module which carries the astronauts and separates from the main vehicle upon launch(it carried astronauts like Kellegerardi in June 2021) and put the first Pakistani woman in space, Namira Salim have sprung up. However, other reports have it that the first Pakistani in space will go into space in 2022 riding piggyback on board a Chinese LM-5 (Long March)-5 rocket. The LM series have also put Pakistan's first two remote sensing satellites into orbit-the PRSS-1 and PRSS-2 and Norah Patten is on course to becoming the first Irish woman in space. Elon Musk also owns the Tesla group of car companies.

IV

The United Kingdom

The British Chief of the General Staff is the military deputy to the Secretary of State for Defense and works alongside the civilian deputy, the Permanent Undersecretary of State for Defense and typically is a member of the Chiefs of Staff Committee which is headed by the senior most of the service Chiefs.

The incumbent British Chief of the General Staff is Gen.Patrick Sanders preceded in that rather coveted position by Gen. Mark Carleton Smith preceded by Gen. Nicholas Christopher 'Nick' Carter, later Chief of Defense Staff. Other British Chiefs of General Staff include Geoffrey Baker, Richard Hull, William Nicholson, John French, Peter Hunt, Admiral Michael Boyce, Gen. Michael Walker, Admiral of the Fleet Michael Boyce and others.

The Chief of Defence Staff

The Chief of Defense Staff nominated by the Secretary of State for Defense and appointed by the Prime Minister with the Queen in Council is the single point military adviser to the Prime Minister. Incidentally, the top general in India earns more in PPP (Purchasing Power Parity) terms than the top general in the United States or the UK.

The incumbent British Chief of Defense Staff is former Chief of Naval Staff and First Sea Lord Admiral Sir Tony Radakin KCB, ADC who is preceded in that position by Gen. Nicholas Christopher 'Nick' Carter preceded by Air Chief Marshal Sir Stuart Peach. The very first Chief of Defense Staff was Neville Littleton, other Chiefs of Defense Staff being Viscount Alan Francis Alan Brooke, Richard Hull, Chief of the Imperial General Staff as the position was known from 1948 to 1964 Gen. William Robert Robertson. Incidentally, Gen. Robertson is the very first British Chief of General Staff.

The Chief of Air Staff

The British Chief of Air Staff is the head of the Royal Air Force, the oldest in the world. The British Chief of Air Staff is the military deputy to the Secretary of State for Defense and like the Chief of General Staff works alongside the civilian deputy, the Permanent Under Secretary of State for Defense. He is typically a member of the Chiefs of Staff Committee.

The present Chief of Air Staff is Air Chief Marshal Sir Michael 'Mike' Wigston OBE, ADC preceded by Air Chief Marshal Stephen John Hillier. Former Chief of Defense Staff Air Chief Marshal Sir Stuart Peach is another Air Chief of the UK. The first British Chief of Air Staff was Major General Hugh Trenchard.

<u>First Sea Lord and Chief of Naval Staff</u>

The Senior Naval Lord to the Board of Admiralty and Chief of Naval Staff, not to be confused with First Lord of the Admiralty and other positions was created in 1684 and the office was changed to First Naval Lord to the Board of Admiralty and Chief of Naval Staff in 1771 and the title was adopted in 1805 and the office was changed to First Sea Lord and Chief of Naval Staff in 1905 with Admiral of the Fleet Sir John Fisher becoming the first First Sea Lord and Chief of Naval Staff. Now the office holder sits on the Defense Council and the Admiralty Board and is a member of the Chiefs of Staff Committee.

The very first Senior Naval Lord and Chief of Naval Staff was Admiral Arthur Herbert and the very first First Naval Lord and Chief of Naval Staff was Admiral Augustus Harvey and they were followed by a long list of office holders like Admiral Sir John Jennings, Admiral John Norris, Admiral Edward Leake, Admiral Francis Holburne, Admiral Charles Saunders, Admiral Archibald Yell, Admiral George Rooke, Lord Augustus Keppel, Admiral George Darby, Earl of Oxford, Earl Howe, Admiral Hugh Palliser, Admiral Thomas Hardy, Lord John Forbes, Admiral John Hay, Admiral James Graham, Admiral James Gambier, Admiral James Martin, Admiral William Martin, Admiral James Dundas, Admiral George Dundas, Admiral William Howe, Admiral Joseph Yorke, Admiral Richard Saunders Dundas, Lord Edward Boscaween, Admiral of the Fleet

Arthur Fredrick Richards, Admiral Anthony Hoskins, Admiral Edward Russel, Admiral of the Fleet Sir John Fisher, Admiral Phillip Andrew Phil Jones who participated in the Falklands War and commanded British warships like H.M.S. Beaver and went to the same military academy as Pakistani Naval Chief Zafar Mehmood Abbasi, the Royal Naval Academy, present CDS Admiral Tony Radakin, KCB, ADC and the incumbent Sir Ben Key KCB, OBE.

The flagship of the English First Sea Lord and Chief of Navy Staff is Horatio, Lord Nelson Sea of the Line, H.M.S. Victory.

The equivalent NATO codes for the British Admiral of the Fleet, a honorary rank, are OF-10 and OF-11.

British Nuclear and Space facilities include High Island, Isle of Man space launch port, Womera rocket testing site in the Australian outback and other launch ports and nuclear testing sites like the former Lancashire, Cambridge nuclear testing site which is now a center for proactively searching for extra-terrestrial life.

V

Russia

The Army

The Russian Chief of the General Staff is Gen. Valery Vasilyevich Gerasimov, a product of Malinovsky Armored Forces Academy and Kazan Military School. A veteran of the war in Dombass and the Syrian War his Deputy, the Russian Deputy Chief of General Staff is Gen. Nikolai Bogdanovsky. The very first Russian Chief of the General Staff and Adjuntant General is Gen. Pavel Gavrilovich Gagarin. The Russian Army dates to the times of the Russian Empire.

The Russian Commander-in-Chief of the Ground Forces

A product of the Malinovsky Armored Forces Academy and the Ulyanovsk Tank School the Russian Commander-in-Chief of the Ground Forces is General of the Army Gen. Leonodovich Ulyanov Salyukov.

The Russian Air Force

The Russian Air Chief is Andrey Yudin. Other Air Chiefs include Andrey Kuznetsov, Sergei Dronov(a product of Gagarin Flight School), and notable Air Chiefs include Viktor Bondarev. On an average, plane for plane, the Russian Air Force is older than most Air Forces in the world.

The Russian Navy

Dating back to the times of the Russian Empire the Russian Navy is commanded by Admiral Nikolai Yevmenov. The Russian Pacific Fleet, headquartered at Murmarnsk, boasts of the world's only nuclear ice breaker fleet.

Commander-in-Chief of The Russian Aerospace Forces

The position was created in 2015 with the clubbing together of the Russian Air Force, Russian Air and Missile Defense Forces and the Space Forces. A product of Frunze Military Academy (2002) and Military School of the Russian Federation and decorated with the Hero of the Russian Federation, Order of Red Star, Order of Merit and Order of Courage (battles wond wars fought include the War in Dombass, regiment is 32nd Motorized Infantry Regiment etc.) but placed on 1 year probation for leaking military secrets, the present Commander-in-Chief of the Russian Aerospace Forces reporting directly to the Chief of the

General Staff is Gen. Sergei Surovkin preceded by Lt. Gen. Acting Pavel Kurachenko, preceded by Gen. Viktor Bondarev(notable commanders).

The Russian Aerospace Forces are responsible for Russia's land-based ICBMs, operation of Russia's military satellites and the Plesetsk Military Cosmodrome in Northwestern Russia. Incidentally, some years back (as of 2021), a Cyclone 3 rocket launched from the Plesetsk Military Cosmodrome exploded and disintegrated over the East Siberian Sea in Russia's Far East carrying with it six satellites, highlighting the risks of keeping nuclear weapons although the incident was not related to nuclear weapons. Also, several years back, Russia and Mongolia inked a pact on the accidental firing of missiles.

Commander-in-Chief of the Russian Space Forces

The Commanders-in-Chiefs of the Russian Space Forces which are responsible for aerospace warfare and to thwart missile attacks from outer space are starting with the very first Lt. Gen. Kerim Kerimov, followed by Lt. Gen. Andrei Karas, Lt. Gen. Vladimir Ivanov, Lt. Gen. Anatoly Perminov, also a Director of ROSCOSMOS, Lt. Gen. Vladimir Alexandrovich Popovkin, also a Director of the Russian Space Agency ROSCOSMOS, Lt. Gen. Oleg Ostapenko who was later promoted to Deputy Defense Minister and who was also a Director of ROSCOSMOS, Lt. Gen Vladimir. M. Ivanov and Lt. Gen Alexander Golovko.

Strategic Missile Forces

In September 2015, the Russian Aerospace Forces and the Russian Space Forces were clubbed together into the Strategic Missile Forces and placed under the command of Gen. Sergei Karakayev, other notable Commanders being Igor Sergeyev, Nikolai Maximov and others. The Svobodny Cosmodrome comes under the purview of the Strategic Missile Forces. The Russian Aerospace Forces and the Russian Space Forces no longer exist.

Strategically important Russian military facilities include the 820B Main Centre for Air and Missile Attack Warning at Solekhnogorsk, the Lekhtusi Radar Station, Zhukov Air and Space Academy and hundreds of other Russian military installations spread across the vast expanse of the Russian Federation. As per satellite imagery and new START US Government sources, Russia has 310 deployed ICBMs with1,189 warheads. The heaviest and most powerful missile in the world is the Russian R-37 M (SS-18, Satan) which belongs to the R-37 family of ICBMs that Russia cold launched in 1971.

Russian plans for the 2020-30s include retaining its non-strategic nuclear arsenal even while modernizing, improving, and reforming its launchers which include two warhead types.

New Russian nuclear submarines include the Borei and Borei-1A Potemkin, the Donstoy, Project 75, 636.3 nuclear submarines and other submarines which are on the an anvil.

Russian Space and Nuclear facilities include the new Voshtoshny Cosmodrome which Russia constructed after Baikanour went to Kazhakastan, Svobodny Cosmodrome, Amur Oblast, Plesetsk Military Cosmodrome in European Russia, the Semipalatinsk nuclear testing site where Russia tested its first atom bomb and hundreds of other Space and

Nuclear facilities spread across the vast expanse of the Russian Federation.

Sunk American and Russian nuclear submarines include the USS Scorpion, USS Thresher, and USS Nautalius and the Russian Kursk which sank in the Barents Sea in the Russian Far East off the Kamchatka peninsula and the Komsomolets.

A rocket has four parts:1)Structural System or frame of the rocket which is similar to the fuselage of an airplane which falls off as the rocket lifts off, 2)Payload System, 3)Guidance System and 4)Propulsion System. Another point to note about rockets is the what is called the Gravity Turn when the rocket inclines itself and places the satellite into orbit.

Coming to satellites, a satellite sends the signal through the Uplink, the Transponder converts the frequency and the Downlink on the ground picks up the signal.

With regard to orbits there are three types of orbits:1)Equatorial Orbit which is aligned at 0 degrees to the Equator, 2)Inclined Orbit-these are all orbits except those aligned over the Equator and at the North and South Poles and 3)Polar Orbits which are those orbits which are aligned over the two poles.

Orbits can also be classified as 1)Circular Orbits and 2)Elliptical Orbits. A thing to remember about Elliptical Orbits is the Perigee point. and the Apogee point. While the Perigee point is where the satellite comes closes to Earth and the Apogee point is where the satellite is farthest away from the Earth.

Satellites are of three types:1)Navigation Satellites which are used for navigation purposes and which have crucial military applications providing crucial military information and input to national leaders, 2)Weather

Satellites which are used for weather forecasting purposes and 3)Communication Satellites which are used to send signals for internet, T.V. and radio purposes.

Four countries in the world have GPS or Global Positioning System which is used for positioning purposes.

They are the American GPS, the Russian GLONASS which India joined in 2010 in a bid by India and Russia to take Indo-Russian cooperation to outer space only for India to later go in for its own GPS, the Indian Regional Navigation Satellite System(IRNSS) or NaVic, a family of 7 satellites which provides positioning services over a region extending 1,500 km from the epicentre and China's Beidou Navigation Satellite System I and II which lifted off from the launchport built at the height of the Sino-Soviet rivalry in the mid-60s, the Wenchang launchport. The BNSS is a family of 30 satellites providing positioning services over such crucial areas as China's BRI Initiative. Following the Sino-Indian hostilities in 2020s, Beidou Map was among 115 Chinese apps to be banned in India along with Cam Scanner, ClubFactory etc dealing a bodyblow to China.

VI
France

The French military matrix

The Chief of Defense Staff (Chef d Etat)

The French Chief of Defense Staff or Chef d Etat, the single point military advisor to the French President, responsible for all French Armed Forces, is former Chief of the Armee De Terre Gen.Thierry Burkhard preceded by Gen. Francois Lecointre. Another French Chief of Defense Staff is Gen. Phillip De Villiers. The inaugural Chef d Etat is Charles Lecheres.

The Chief of Army Staff (Armee De Terre)

The French Chief of Army Staff is Gen.Pierre Shill reporting to the Chief of Defence Staff or Chef d Etat preceded by Gen. Thierry Burkhard now Chef d Etat..

The Chief of Air Staff (Armee De Aire)

The French Chief of Air Staff is Air Force General Stephanie Mille preceded by Air Force Gen. Andre Lanata. Two former Air Chiefs are the incumbent's predecessor Air Force Gen. Phillippe Lavigne who recently (2020) paid a visit to the French aerospace giant Dassault's headquarters in Paris as Air Chief to assess France's fighter preparedness and Air Force Gen. Dennis Mitchell.

The Chief of Naval Staff

The French Chief of Naval Staff is Admiral Pierre Vandier responsible for deployment of all French Naval Forces who is preceded by Admiral Christophe Prazuck.

French nuclear and rocket testing Sites include the Murora Atoll in the South Pacific, Ille Du Levalt rocket launching site and other sites.

VII
China

The Chinese military apex is headed by the Chief of General Staff, the top general in China. The present Chief of General Staff is Gen. Huang Shu Kuang. The first Chief of General Staff was Marshal Su Yu. Other Chinese Chiefs of General Staff include Gen.Feng Fenghui, Gen. Chi Haotian, Gen. X, Gen. Cao Gangchuan, Gen. Liang Guanglie, Gen. Chang Wanquan and others.

The Chief of Army Staff

The Chinese Chief of Army Staff is Gen. Han Weiguo. His predecessor is Gen. Li Zuocheng (now Chief of Joint Staff in the Central Military Commission), political commissar, Li Liwei. The Chinese Chief of PLA Staff during the Sino-Indian War of 1962 was Gen. Luo Ruishing(1959-65) who secured for Communist China such a key victory in the war that it was not until Battle 2020 that a resurgent India finally began to reverse some of the gains the Chinese secured during the war. Some of India's gains, wrangled on the negotiating table, include in Tangang Tso where both countries are in an advantage and Demchok and the Hot Springs region where the Chinese are at an advantage. However, the Chinese are not fools, and they extracted their own gains like in the Depsang region before conceding ground in a deal hammered out between the two countries at the end of Battle 2020. Incidentally, the outgoing US Ambassador Kenneth. I. Juster (who was followed by Charge D' Affairs Donald.L.Heflin who in turn was followed by Charge D' Affairs Edgard. D. Kagan to be followed by Charge D' Affairs Daniel. Bennet. Smith, Daniel.B.Smith, Charge D'.Affairs Patricia.A.Lacina and Charge.D.Affairs A.Elizabeth Beth Jones. She was followed by the new current US Ambassador to India Eric Garcetti) confirmed that the U.S. was active in Ladakh during the recent India-China standoff but when pressed on the exact nature of the U.S. coordination he declined to comment leaving the onus of disclosure on the Indian government. He, however, claimed no country does more than his country for the security of Indians and India as India faces growing Chinese restiveness perhaps on a continuing basis. Sure enough as if to prove the US Ambassador's words true there are again rumblings across the Himalayas with 30 fighter jets of the Chinese Air Force (CAF) conducting aerial exercises at Chinese Air Bases like Kashgar, Hotan, and Ngari Gunsa off Eastern Ladakh near the Indian border in June 2021. Other important Air Bases where the CAF is showing activity include Shigatse, Lhasa Gongkar, Nyingchi and Chamdo Pangta. In response to this new Chinese military activity, India has activated its fighter aircraft fleet, including the Rafale jets on its northern borders in keeping with its heightened state of military preparedness in these areas and is keeping a close surveillance. Also, the CAF and the PAF held joint aerial exercises at an operational airfield in Pakistan's Sindh province while special troops from India and Kyrgyzstan held Operation Khanjar, and Pakistan held Pabbi Anti-Terrorism under the aegis of the Shanghai Cooperation Organization. Also, the U.S. Ambassador accompanied by the U.S. Military Attache` in New Delhi Rear Admiral Eileen Haskins Laubacher, Eileen. H. Laubacher called on the then Army Chief Gen. Manoj Mukund Naravane, Gen. M.M. Naravane before the U.S. Ambassador's departure from the host country. In the negotiations, India's Northern Command led by General-officer-Commanding-in- Chief (GOC-in-C), Northern Command Gen. Yogesh Kumar Joshi played a key role, and the Chinese side was led by its Commander-in-Chief of its Western Theatre Ground Force Gen. Xu Quiling among others. Incidentally, as China's first Minister of Public Security (1954-59) Gen. Luo Ruishing played a key role in the shaping of China's police and security apparatus, a key appendage in Communist China. He died in Heidelberg in what was then West Germany. Throughout the period between 1962 and 2020, there was regular attrition of Indian territory by the Chinese.

The Chief of Air Staff

The Chinese Chief of Air Staff is Air Force General Chang Dingqui preceded by Ding Laihang who in turn was preceded by Air Force General Ma Xiaotian. Other Chinese Air Chiefs include Air Force General Xu Quiliang, Ma Ning and others. The Chinese Air Force saw action during the Korean War.

The Chief of Naval Staff

The Chinese Chief of Naval Staff is Admiral Dong Jun preceded by Zhang Wendan preceded by Admiral Shen Jinlong, among others.

The Rocket Forces

Until 2016 the 2nd Artillery Command, the Chinese Rocket Forces which participated in the Third Taiwan Straits crisis are led by Gen. Li Yuchao who is preceded by Gen. Jing Haiping. Incidentally, China is making its nuclear arsenal leaner and meaner in response to U.S. moves in the Asia-Pacific.

The Strategic Support Force

The Chinese Strategic Support Force Commanders-in-Chief include Gen.Ji Qiansheng preceded by Gen. Gao Jin and others while political commissars include the present Li Liwei, Wang Jiashen and others.

Apart from the Chinese weapons already mentioned by this author in his India-China Balance of Power (Balance of Terror?) article, weapons in the Chinese inventory include the Ming class submarine in which 11 sailors were killed when there was an oxygen leak, the Jin class submarine, and the Han class submarine. There is also the J-10 stealth bomber and China recently unveiled a top-class drone and India, in response, bought out a drone which bears an uncanny resemblance to one of its South Korean counterparts.

Chinese Rocket Testing Sites

Chinese Rocket Testing include Base 603, Shiejiedu, Guangde, Xicheng Rocket Testing Site constructed at the height of the Sino-Soviet rivalry in the 60s, Wenchang Rocket Testing Site, Jiuquan Rocket Launching Station in the Gobi Desert, Northwestern China, and others. Chinese Nuclear testing sites include Lop Nor, where China exploded its first atom bomb in 1964.

On December 3, 1941, Enrico Fermi and his team of scientists created the world's first self-sustaining nuclear chain reaction and ushered in the Nuclear Age. America which now has the Nuclear Regulatory and Development Establishment(NRDE) under the Secretary of Energy with oversight over America's nuclear activities, peaceful and otherwise, did have an Atomic Energy Commission(AEC) from 1948 to 1974, with headquarters at German Town, Maryland, Washington D.C., when it was disbanded following a public outcry over radioactive iodine-133 and Xenon-131 experiments on pregnant women and babies in Iowa, New Hampshire and other parts of the United States and America's nuclear activities were dovetailed under the NRDE.

The first Chairman of the AEC was David. E. Lilienthal, followed by Gordon Dean, a lawyer, Lewis. W. Strauss, John. A. McCone, Glenn. T. Seaborg (a Nobel Laureate on whom the Enrico Fermi Award was also conferred), James. T. Schlesinger, also the first Secretary of Energy and Dixy Lee

Ray, the only woman to helm the AEC. The father of the atom bomb, Dr, Robert. J. Oppenheimer (a member of the Communist Party of America), as the Chairman of the General Advisory Committee gave one of the most controversial pieces of advice in United States history-that the United States continue to produce atom bombs instead of going in for hydrogen bombs as they were considered too destructive to have any military potential. This led to the United States losing the race to produce the world's first hydrogen bomb to the U.S.S.R. which detonated the world's first hydrogen bomb in 1948 in Semipalatinsk in Russia. Later President Eisenhower overruled Oppenheimer's advice and the United States detonated its first hydrogen bomb in the Central Pacific Proving Grounds on Nov.1, 1952. This coupled with Oppenheimer's membership of the American Communist Party in a sea of capitalism led to his later side lining on the insistence of AEC Chairmen like Lewis. W. Strauss and Senator Brien McMahon. In fact, McMahon got Oppenheimer removed from the General Advisory Committee. Later, as a compensation, Dr. Oppenheimer was conferred the Enrico Fermi Award. Also, Strauss's arrogance and condescending attitude towards Congress cost him the Senate seat.

Director of ROSATOM, Russia's apex nuclear body, is Alexei Levatich preceded by Sergei Kirilenko. Britain's United Kingdom Atomic Energy Authority is headed by Ian Chapman, preceded by Sir David Gann CBE. Former Chairmen include Sir Stephen Charles Cowley Feng Flnstp, a fusion expert and an international authority on fusion, France Alternative Energies and Atomic Energy Commission Chief is Francois Jacq. Former Chairmen include Daniel Viverde, Bernard Bigot, and others. High Commissioner for Atomic Energy is Yves Brecht. China's

Atomic Energy Authority is headed by Director Liu Yongde and Secretary General Xu Dazhe. Pakistan's Atomic Energy Commission is chaired by Mohammed Naeem and finally the incumbent Chairman of India's Atomic Energy Commission is

Dr. Kamlesh Neelkanth Vyas, preceded by Dr. Shekhar Basu, Dr. Ratan Kumar Sinha, R.K. Sinha, Dr. Sri Kumar Banerjee, Dr. Anil Kakodkar, Dr. Raja Ramanna, Dr. Malur Ramaswamy Srinivasan, M. R. Srinivasan, a mechanical engineer who played a key role in the construction of the PHwR or Pressurized Heavy Water Reactor, Dr. H.N. Sethna, Dr. Vikram Sarabhai and the first Chairman, Homi Jehangir Homi Bhabha. India has till date 7 atomic power stations. They are the latest addition, Narora nuclear power plant, Ghaziabad, Rawatbhatta, Kaiga, Kakrapar, The Russian assisted Kudankulam nuclear power plant in Tamil Nadu, Kalpakkam, also in Tamil Nadu, the Tarapur Atomic Power Station (Taps) where scientists watch computer screens as billions of megawatts of electricity blitzes out of the American assisted Tarapur Atomic Power Station. Perhaps, nowhere else do the lines between old and new get blurred as in India. For e.g., you may find a man reciting a 3,000 year old prayer before beginning work in an atomic energy plant. Let the TIME magazine cover story "India enters the nuclear age on a bullock cart" way back in the 50s at the time of India's American assisted Taps Apsara reactor carry the day. However, thankfully, bullock carts are long since a thing of the past in the vastly changed India of today. However, the future belongs to fusion and the world should heavily invest in fusion as it offers unlimited potential. Recently, the large fusion reactor in South West China reproduced the Sun's power here on Earth.

America's NASA Administrators include the incumbents, Steve Jurcyk and Bill Nelson, James Fredrick 'Jim' Bridenstine, Major Charles Bolden, Robert Lahmer, James. C. Green, James C. Webb after whom the James Webb Space Telescope is named, Thomas O. Payne, Fredrick Gregory and others. Chief Scientists include the inuagural holder Thomas Keith Glennan, Noel Hinner, Katie Olson, John Galvin, Ellen Stofen and others.

Directors of Russia's space agency, ROSCOSMOS include the incumbent Dmitri Rogozin, his predecessor, Igor Komarov, Oleg Ostapenko, Vladimir Alexandrovich Popovkin, Anatoly Perminov, and the very first Director Yuri Koptev.

Director of UK space agency is Graham Turnock and Tang Denjie is the chief of China National Space Administration while Jean Yves Le Gall is the Director of France's Aeriales Spaces Nationale, France's space Agency.

Pakistan's Space and Upper Atmospheres Research Commission (SUPARCO) which notched up some successes esp. in the initial years of its existence like the Rehbar expendable first stage production rocket and the BADAR I and II satellites has in later years been dogged by military and bureaucratic hassles and interference and has of late been led by rather lacklusture, uniformed figures like Major General Riaz Hussein, Major Gen. Bilal Akbar, Major Gen. Qaiser Annes Khurram, the present Amir Nadeem and others. This is in contrast to the distinguished figures like Dr. Abdus Salam, Air Commodore Dr. Salim Mahmud, Air Commodore Dr. Wladislaw Turowicz, Dr. Engineer Zaman, Shafi Rehman, Muhammed Ahmed and others who helmed SUPARCO in its initial years. The agency has come under fire within Pakistan of not being able to stand up to its Chinese and Indian couinterparts.

Coming to India's ISRO the various Directors who led it in its distinguished years of existence (in sharp contrast to SUPARCO) are starting with the first (in fact SUPARCO which was formed In 1961 Is 8 years older than ISRO which was formed in on August 15, 1969) the father of the Indian space program, Dr. Vikram Sarabhai, Dr. Satish Dhawan, Dr.M.G.K.Menon who held the post for only 6 months, Dr. Madhavan Nair, Dr. Udupi Ramchandra Rao, U. R. Rao who is rated among the top 10 space personalities of the world, Dr. Krishnaswamy Kasturirangan, Dr.K.Kasturirangan, Dr.Shailesh Nayak, Dr. K.Radhakrishnan who said "talent grows in silent places", Dr.A.S.Kiran Kumar, "rocket man" of India, Dr. Kailasadivu Sivan, K.Sivan, the present senior rocket engineer, Dr.S.Somnath who is also Secretary, Department of Space(DoS).

Crucial ISRO facilities include 1)Vikram Sarabhai Space Centre, Thiruvanthapuram, 2)Satish Dhawan Space Centre, Sriharikota, 3)ISRO Propulsion Complex, Mahendragiri, 4)Space Applications Centre(SAC), Ahmedabad, 5)Indian Remote Sensing Centre, Hyderabad, 6)ISRO Telemetry, Tracking and Command Centre(ISTRACK), Thiruvanthapuram, and 7)Liquid Propulsion Systems Centre, Valiamala, Thiruvanthapuram and 8)the Inertial Systems Unit, Thiruvanthapuram. Most of these facilities are sitting ducks for Chinese Dong Feng-28 ICBMs stationed in Tibet which are trained on to peninsular India. This is a point worth pondering over for the Indian government.

ISRO missions include Chandrayaan I, the ill fated Chandrayaan II which did however manage to put the Indian tricolour on the moon, Mangalyaan and astronomical mission ASTROSAT I.

Upcoming missions include India's solar probe, Aditya L1, NASA, ISRO collaboration mission NARS, India's Venus probe Shukriyaan I, Gaganyaan which was slated to have been launched in December 2021 but will be launched no earlier than 2024 and ASTROSAT II.

Important dates to remember with regard to ISRO include ISRO's formation date, August 15, 1969 a few full 8 years after SUPARCO was formed, on October 9, 1971 India's first sounding rocket Rohini-125, a small sounding rocket was launched, on August 10, 1979 the first of the SLV series SLV-1 was launched with the last SLV-4 being launched on April 17, 1983. Another important date to remember is when India's workhorse rocket PSLV was launched on September 20th, 1993, the first of India's GSLV series of Mark I configuration was launched on April18[th], 2001 but it was a failure but the second developmental flight achieved all the parameters. Chandrayaan I who found evidence of water bodies on the moon was launched on October 22, 2008 while the Mangalyaan mission was launched on November 5, 2013. Chandrayaan II was launched on July 22, 2019 while India's mission to send Gaganauts who are undergoing training at the Gagarin Flight School, Moscow, Russia or its own astronauts to space who will go to space abroad a brute of a indigenous vehicle, the Bahubali rocket was originally slated to take place in December 2021 but will now take place no earlier than 2024.

VIII

Saudi Arabia-The Power Paradigm in the Middle East

The Chief of the General Staff of Saudi Arabia is Air Chief Marshal Fayyad Bin Hamad bin Rawad Al Ruwaili (who is also the Chief of the Royal Saudi Air Forces and Chief of Joint Staff). Other Saudi Chiefs of General Staff include Gen. Hamad bi Mohammad Al Shammery, the incumbent's predecessor, Field Marshal Abdul Rehman bin Khan Al Banyan, Field Marshal Mohammed bin Saleh Al Muhaya (who had experience in the Gulf War and the conflict in Yemen), Col. Jafer bek Pilot and others.

The Chief of Royal Saudi Land Forces is Prince Fahd Al Saud. The Chief of the Royal Saudi Navy is Admiral Fahd bin Abdullah Al Ghifaili. The Chief of the Royal Saudi Army(COAS) is Gen.Abdullah bin Mohammed Al Sultan preceded by Gen. Abdul Rehman bin Khan Al Banyan who was sacked in a royal purge that took the heads of many including Princes, senior military officers and one prominent businessman Abdul Waheed Al Talal while the Chief of the Royal Saudi Air Forces as we have seen earlier is Air Chief Marshal Fayyad Bin Hamad bin Rawad Al Ruwaili preceded by Air Chief Marshal Mohammed Al Oteib.

Saudi Arabia sources most of its military hardware from its principal ally, the United States as also France, some of it being sourced from Russia, European countries, and other countries like Sweden. A small part of it is indigenously manufactured. The Royal Saudi Army (with headquarters at Al Wazarat, King's Road, Riyadh) is equipped with hardware like the American MI Abrams Tank, M113 armored personnel carriers (APCs), anti-tank missiles include the Russian 9M Kornet, American FGS 113, MBT LAW BILL 2 etc. Assault rifles like the Swiss Stigler and weapons for Artic Patrol Warfare, Attack Helicopters like the Black Hawk Sikorsky also form part of the Saudi inventory. Further, Saudi rank insignia and equivalent NATO codes are as follows-

<u>Sargent Corporal till General</u>

Jundi Jundi Awal

The Royal Saudi Air Forces are equipped with fighter aircraft like the American F-15 Eagle and the Panava Tornado, attack aircraft like the F-15C, trainer aircraft like the PC-9A Pilatus and the British BAE Hawk and transport aircraft like the American C-130 Hercules also form part of the desert kingdom Air Force's armory.

The small Royal Saudi Navy (with headquarters at Al Wazarat, King's Road, Riyadh) has two fleets, the Eastern Fleet based at military bases like Dammam and Ras

Mishab on the eastern seacoast and the Western Fleet based at Jeddah on the Western Coast. It is equipped with 7 frigates, destroyers, and corvettes (a small escort ship). All in all, the Saudi Navy has 300 ships and 50 aircraft.

Incidentally, in the context of the Big Powers, the Washington Treaty of 1922 for the Limitation of Naval Armaments was the outstanding example of a Treaty compounded in success and failure. While it could agree on capital ships, agreement could not be reached on frigates, corvettes, and destroyers. In the context of military treaties, it is worth noting that disagreements can arise while drawing parity between the military forces of various countries like for e. g. how many French colonials are equal to how many German panzer divisions etc.

IX

India-The Royal Bengal Tiger

The Indian military superstructure is apexed by the apex Chief of Defense Staff, a post which fell vacant after Gen. Bipin Rawat (India's first and only CDS till date who belongs to the 11, Gorkha Rifles) died in a helo accident alongwith 14 others. The hunt for a new CDS is on with Army Chief Manoj Mukund Naravane who 2021 became Chairman of the Chiefs of Staff Committee(CCS) understood to be the front runner for the coveted job and other contenders include the Chairman of the Integrated Staffs Committee and the Chairman of the Joint Staffs Committee. But, a dark horse could emerge. And did in the form of Lt.Gen.(retd) Anil Chauhan, former G-o-in-C, Eastern Command. Before the appointment of a CDS, two officers, Lt.Gen.Manoj Pande and Lt.Gen. C.Ponappa were promoted to Dy.Chief of Army staff rank status. And in an important development, in a quick promotion, Lt.Gen Manoj Pande, a former GOC-in-C of the operationally sensitive Eastern Command in moving full throttle and is in cruise mode to be the next Army Chief and indeed he presently became. He will be the first Engineer to helm the Indian Army.

The CDS is assisted by the three service chiefs (who along with the Cabinet Secretary and the Chairman, Atomic Energy Commission form the *Pancha Ratnas* or 5 jewels of India) Chief of Army Staff (COAS), currently Gen. Manoj Pande preceded by Gen. Manoj Mukund Naravane (who belongs to the Sikh Light Infantry), Chief of Air Staff(CAS), currently Air Chief Marshal Vivek Ram Chaudri, V.R.Chaudri and the Chief of Naval Staff (CNS in Indian Navy cables and communications), currently Admiral R. Hari Kumar.

The various Chiefs of Army Staff spread over the years include the very first Army Chief, Gen. Rajendrasinghji Jadeja, the incumbent's predecessor, Lt. Gen. Dalbir Singh Suhag, Gen. Bikram Singh, Gen. Joginder Jaswant Singh, J.J.Singh(later Arunachal Pradesh Governor), Gen Sundarajan Padmanabhan(Paddy to his colleagues), the 'thinking General' Gen. Krishnaswamy Sundarji, K. Sundarji (a product of Defense Services Staff College, Wellington, Tamil Nadu, where he settled after retirement), the present Minister of State for Road Transport and Highways, former Minister of State for External Affairs and North Eastern Affairs and 5 time Ghaziabad MP, Gen. Vijendra Kumar Singh, V.K.Singh(who like former Director General, ISI Naveed Mukhtar Chaudhary is a product of the elite Army War College, Carlyle, West Virginia, United States), the distinguished Gen. Ved Pratap Mullick, V.P. Mullick who led India to victory during the Kargil War (but not before Pakistani forces penetrated embarrassingly deep into Indian territory and a request went out from Army Headquarters to Air Headquarters, Vayu Bhavan, for Air Force "help" and it was left to then Air Chief, Air Chief Marshal Anil Yashwant Tipnis to remind the Army that "help" in a democracy like India had to be routed through civilian quarters), Gen Shankar Rai Choudhary, Gen. K.V. Krishna Rao (later Jammu and Kashmir and Mizoram Governor apart from holding various other important positions), Gen. A.S. Vaidya (of Operation Blue Star fame who along with Indira Gandhi was assassinated for his role in cleaning up the Golden Temple of terrorists holed up inside the temple. Interestingly, the first few brave officers and soldiers who formed the 'spearhead arm' of Operation Blue Star knew they were sitting ducks for the first volley of bullets from the terrorists' side and knew they would be instantly killed as they led the Operation), Gen. Jayantho Nath Chaudri, J. N. Chaudri, Gen. Deepak Kapoor, Gen. Nirmal Kumar Vij, Gen. Gopal Gurunath Bewoor, Gen. Gopalaswamy Kumarmangalam, the very first Commander-in-Chief of the Indian Army, Field Marshal 'Kipper' Madappa Cariappa who was born on Jan 28th, 1895, in Sarawanasanthe, Karnataka and died in Bangalore in 1993, Gen. Thimmayya, and who can, of course, forget the famous and legendary Gen. Sam Hormusji Fateh Manekshaw, Gen. S.H.F.J.Manekshaw as he led to the Indian Army, the second largest in the world (as per some accounts it now ranks 4th having lost the 2nd and 3rd position to the U.S. Army and the Russian Army) to victory during the Indo-Pak War of 1971 (interestingly, Gen. Manekshaw was so impressed by the bravery of one particular Pakistani soldier during the war that he later recommended to the Pakistani Government that he be suitably rewarded. In his words "I do not know if they held it out against him, but

I did do so.) and other distinguished officers. Gen. Manekshaw, of course, occupies a special place in India's history, heart, and Indians' heart. Of him, it was said "Play again Sam" as he "faded away".

Coming to the IAF, which ranks among the 10 greatest Air Forces of the world, the incumbent Chief of Air Staff is Air Chief Marshal Vivek Ram Chaudri, V.R.Chaudri who took charge after Air Chief Marshal Rakesh Kumar Singh Bhadauria R.K.S. Bhadauria demitted office. Air Chief Marshal Bhadauria is preceded by Air Chief Marshal (retd.) Birendra Singh Dhanoa (whose initials B.S. are engraved on to the tail fins of the Tejas fighter aircraft in cognizance of his monumental contribution to the Indian Air Force. He was the Air Chief during the 2016 surgical strikes against Pak terror dens), who in turn is preceded by Air Chief Marshal Arup Kumar Raha preceded by Air Chief Marshal Norman Anil Kumar Browne, Air Chief Marshal N.A.K.Browne. Other Air Chiefs include Air Chief Marshal Anil Yashwant Tipnis who as a young pilot officer during the 1971 Indo-Pak War was so awe struck by a Pakistani American made F-104 Starfighter(which has since headed for the Smithsonian) that in his own words "failed to open fire". Of course, things are very different today with America long since de-hyphenating a resurgent India and Pakistan. Problem for India is that Pakistan occupies a geographically strategic place.

Nevertheless, America or for that matter any power has little interest in small fry Pakistan today and India too should shed its Pakistan obsession and zero in on China as India competes to place itself at the global high table and China too regards India as its rival and competitor, not friend. In this connection, Wharton's Geoffrey Garett feels as to the question whether India [which recently became the sixth largest financial arrangement edging out France and Italy to 7th place and 8th place respectively and is now dead heat with Europe's second largest economy, the UK which it will overtake in 2023 and has since overtaken and emerged as the fifth largest financial arrangement in the world edging out its erstwhile colonizer to sixth place and had it not been but for the scourge of the parallel economy and compromised currency, would have vied for the 4th spot with Germany but thanks to India's polished and other *chors*, the country has to rest content playing second fiddle (however, for a country of India's size and dimensions, rather than the size of its economy, the true measure of economic performance is GDP averaged to gross per capita income and here India fares rather poorly compared to even small countries like Qatar, Macau, Singapore, Ireland, Taiwan and the like, but so does China. Also something which doesn't fit well with the fact that India today has at long last found the economic status concomitant with its status as a major economy is the fact that 8 Indian states have poverty levels more in tune with that of Sub-Saharan Africa than with that of a first world economy that India today supposedly is.

However, a caveat here. Developing small countries is easy while developing unwieldy giants like India and China is not. However, it averages out.)] can be the next China two answers are yes and one maybe. To elaborate, China, like the United States and Japan, has serious demographic demons, for e. g. China will be old before it is rich whereas in India's case, the mean age is 35 years with 65% of the population below the age of 35 years. However, China has built on infrastructure, investment, and manufacturing while India has barely scratched the surface on all three. On balance, Indian democracy is beyond vibrant, while China is one party state. To sum up, India will be next China only if it makes the answer to the second question also yes, otherwise no.

The revised updated list of the world's top 10 economies is as follows:1)United States 2)China 3)Japan 4)Germany 5)India 6)Britain 7)France 8)Italy 9)Canada and 10)South Korea and Brazil which are tied for the tenth spot. And according to a UN report all this will radically change by 2050 when India will emerge as the world's second largest economy edging out the United States to third position and India will be just behind China which by that time will emerge on top of the charts. And look beyond 2050 and you will realize that from then on it will be India's tryst with destiny as India once again assumes pole position and becomes the "*sone ki chidiya*" that it was in the days of yore. And what's more, India's notional GDP will surpass that of the United States in the year 2075. Already former CEO of ANZ Grindlays Bank Michael Smith noted India was looking more and more like the jewel in the crown and it was a mistake to withdraw from India which Deutsch Bank's Christian Sewing recently said India was a shining star amid global turmoil.

Again according to an IMF report, the top 10 economies in the world in terms nominal GDP at current US $ exchange rates are as follows:1)USA 2)China, 3)Japan, 4)Germany, 5)India 6)Britain 7)France 8)Italy 9)Canada and 10)South Korea and Brazil which are tied for the tenth spot. And in PPP(Purchasing Power Parity) terms India with $10 trillion is just behind China with $27 trillion and America with $23 trillion. Also, India is poised to overtake Britain, its erstwhile coloniser, as the fifth largest financial arrangement in the world in 2023(which as we have seen earlier it has since did) and Japan as Asia's second largest financial arrangement in 2030. According to other figures, India in now a $ 3.1 trillion economy. Drawing up level with first world economies is definitely a game changer.

However, is India now a first world economy?. Union Minister Nitin Gadkari says India is a rich country with poor people. It faces issues of poverty, unemployment, casteism, untouchability etc as it prepares to foist itself at the global high table. Another fact which doesn't fit well with India's new found status as a first world economy is the fact that as many as 8 states languishing in Sub-Saharan poverty and India is pretty low on the world's "Serious Hunger" list.

However, things are changing fast with even backward states like U.P. and Bihar surging ahead.The world will indeed look very different in 2050. For e.g. a present day first world economy, France will no longer rank among the top ten economies of the world then.

Also, a purpotedly related fact is that the traditionally skewed sex ratio obtaining in India has been reversed. It now stands at every 1020 women to 1000 men. The tipping point has been reached remarkably fast thanks to a crackdown on sex determination tests and we are now, indeed, in the centrifuge of change. The current ranking of the world's most populous countries is 1)China 2)India 3)United States. But, the gap between the first two and the third is very large. But, all this will radically change in 2025 when India will emerge as the world's most populous nation edging out China to second position while the United States will remain at third position.

Coming back to the topic of India's Air Chiefs, other Indian Air Chiefs include the scandal tainted (the Italian Finmeccanica scandal) Air Chief Marshal S.P.Tyagi, the only helicopter pilot to become Air Chief, Air Chief Marshal Pradeep Vasant Naik, Air Chief Marshal P.V.Naik, Air Chief Marshal Idriss Hassan Latif, Air Chief Marshal I.H.Latif, later Maharashtra Governor and Indian High Commissioner to Canada, Air Chief Marshal Dilbagh Singh, Air Chief Marshal Air Chief Marshal Sundarraman Neelakantan, Air Chief Marshal MSD Wollen, Air Chief during the 1971 Indo-Pak War, Air Chief Marshal Pratap Chandra Lal, Air Chief Marshal P.C.Lal, DFC, Distinguished Flying Cross, the very first Air Chief, the England educated Air Chief Marshal Subroto Mukherjee DFC and the only Marshal of the Air Force Arjan Singh who died 2018. The Naval equivalent, The Admiral of the Fleet rank has not been given to anyone. Notable battles and wars in which the Indian Air Force participated include the 1971 Indo-Pak War, Operation Meghdoot etc.

Coming to the Indian Navy, the very first Chief of Naval Staff was Admiral William Edward Parry who was followed by Admiral Charles Thomas Mark Pizey to be followed by Admiral Stephen Hope Carlill, who, in turn was followed by Admiral Sadashiv Bhoman Mullick, Admiral Adhar Kumar Chatterjee and Admiral Sardarilal Mathradas Nanda, Admiral S. M. Nanda who was at the helm during the 1971 Indo-Pak War and who presided over the bombing of

Karachi harbor during the war. Other Indian Naval Chiefs include the present CNS Admiral R. Hari Kumar, his predecessor Karambir Singh, his predecessor Admiral Sunil Lanba, Admiral Robin Kumar Dhowan, Admiral Devendra Kumar Joshi (currently Andaman and Nicobar Islands Lt. Governor), Admiral Suresh Verma whose nephew Ravi Verma was wanted in the Naval War Room leak case and last heard was a fugitive in London, Admiral Vishnu Bhagwat who was sacked by the Vajpayee government. One of the finest naval visionaries in the world, he went down with his guns blazing writing a book bringing out the skeletons in the Vajpayee government's cupboard. Notable battles and wars in which the Indian Navy participated include the 1971 Indo-Pak War, Operation Cactus etc.

The Operational Commanders

The Army

The Indian Army has 7 Commands. They are,

<u>Eastern Command</u>

Coming to the operational commanders, the General-Officer- Commanding-in-Chief, GOC-in-C, of the operationally sensitive Eastern Command with headquarters at Fort William, Kolkata with oversight over Arunachal Pradesh, Meghalaya, Mizoram, Assam, Manipur, Sikkim and West Bengal, which has delivered many Army

Chiefs in the past including the present Army Chief Gen. Manoj Mukund Naravane, Gen. M. M. Naravane who belongs to the Sikh Light Infantry, commanded a battalion of Rajputana Rifles up the slopes of Jammu and Kashmir and was posted as Military Attache` in Myanmar, incumbent is Gen.Rana Pratap Kalita preceded by Gen. Anil Chauhan, the last Chief of Defense Staff the late Gen. Bipin Rawat, an infantry specialist who belongs to 11, Gorkha Rifles and who was selected over many others like the highly respected and professional Gen. Praveen Bakshi, a armored corps. specialist, Gen. P. M. Hariz, GOC-in-C, Southern Command and others as India was in need of a infantry specialist in view of the counter-insurgency operations facing the country. Gen. Bakshi, however, chose to remain GOC-in-C, Eastern Command.

The Army is divided into three branches- infantry, foot soldiers, armored corps. which is more traditional warfare with the help of tanks, and artillery, Bofors Guns. The majority of Army Chiefs, 18 including the present, have been from the infantry while 6 have been from the armored corps. and 5 have been from the artillery. It is the Infantry man who pushes the enemy out of his bunker and forces him to accept defeat. There are 5 different types of infantry-1)Infantry, 2)Mechanized Infantry, 3)Mountain Infantry, 4)Airborne Infantry and 5)Naval Infantry or Marines. In armoured warfare, armoured tanks and armoured fighting vehicles are also used. As for the artillery, it is the job of field artillery to provide support to other arms esp. in long distance firing.

Notable GOC-in-Cs, Eastern Command are Gen. Dalbir Singh Suhag, Gen. Arun Sridhar Vaidya, Gen. A. S. Vaidya, Gen. Gopalaswamy Kumarmangalam, Gen. Srinivasapuram Krishnaswamy, and of course, the legendary S. H. F. J.

Manekshaw and many, many others.

Northern Command

The GOC-in-C, Northern Command, with headquarters at Udhampur, is Gen. Upendra Dwivedi preceded by Yogesh Kumar Joshi. Notable GOC-in-Cs, Northern Command are Gen. Ranbir Singh, the face of the Army during the surgical strikes of 2016 which made potpouri of the traditional theory that anybody who thought the Indian Army could go in hot pursuit of terrorists holed up in Pakistan was chasing a chimera as it chipped away at Pak terror dens and lairs and who briefed the country's top brass prior to the surgical strikes, in fact, Gen. Singh was among the 5 people shortlisted for the Army Chief's post before Gen. M. M. Naravane clinched the cliffhanger, Gen. Deepak Kapoor, Gen. Sundararajan Padmanabhan, Gen. N. N. Vohra, later a Governor of Jammu and Kashmir and Union Home Secretary, Gen. H.S. Panag who played a rather important role during the talks with China following the armed skirmishes and melee of 2020 and others.

Southern Command

The Southern Command with headquarters at Pune, is a formation which has existed since 1885 as part of the British Indian Army and after Independence became part of the Indian Army. It played a key role during the Goa Liberation War and the integration of several princely states. The GOC-in-C, Southern Command is Gen. J.S. Nain, a highly decorated General preceded by Gen. Chandi Prasad Mohanty. Notable Commanders include Field Marshal K. M. 'Kipper' Madappa Cariappa who was born on Jan. 28,

1885, in Saravanasanthe in what is modern day Karnataka and died in Bangalore in 1993, C. M. Candeth, Gen. Bipin Rawat, Gen. Nirmal Kumar Vij, Gen. N. K. Vij and others.

Western Command

The GOC-in-C, Western Command, with headquarters at Chandi Mandir, Himachal Pradesh, is Gen.Nav.K.Khanduri. Other GOC-in-Cs, Western Command include R.P. Singh AVSM, UYSM, SM.

Central Command

The GOC- in- Cs, of the Lucknow based Central Command include the incumbent Gen. Yogesh Dimri. Other GOC-in-Cs include Iqroop Singh Ghuman and others.

South-Western Command

The GOC-in-C of the Jaipur based South- Western Command is Gen. Amardeep Singh Bhinder preceded by Alok Singh Kler, Gen. A. S. Kler. Gen. Kler, however, had to weather a storm even before took charge as he bicycled all the way from New Delhi to Jaipur to pick up his new posting. The Army top brass frowned upon this commenting that taking charge of a new posting was no time to demonstrate one's penchant for a fitness regimen. He was preceded as GOC-in-C by Gen. Satinder Kumar Sinha, Gen. S. K. Sinha, and others.

One previous Deputy Chief of Army Staff was Gen. D. Anbu

Army Training Command

The GOC-in-C of the backwater Army Training Command is Gen. S.S.Mahal. Others include Cheruvanda Thimayya who took the baton from present Army Chief Gen. Manoj Mukund Naravane, Gen. M. M. Naravane who in a game of musical chairs played with the top brass quantum leaped from the Army Training Command to the Eastern Command before pole vaulting to the top job.

The Air Force

Western Air Command

The Air Officer Commanding-in-Chief, AOC-in-C, Western Air Command which is the IAF's 'sword arm' with 16 Air Bases responsible for aerial defense of North India including India's highest Air Base, Hindon Air Base, Ghaziabad located at a height of over 420 ft. and responsible for aerial defense of Delhi and including over 200 bases under his command is Air Marshal Amit Dev who is preceded by Air Marshal Balakrishnan Suresh who in turn was preceded by Air Marshal Chandrashekhar Hari Kumar who was sacked from his job, Air Marshal Satinder Kumar Sinha and Air Marshal Vivek Ram Chaudri, V.R. Chaudri, now Air Chief. Other notable AOC-in-Cs, Western Air Command, include Air Marshal Anil Raghunath Nambiar, hero of Tiger Hill bombing, who in a move that raised eyebrows was superseded for the Air Chief's post.

Eastern Air Command

AOC-in-Cs, Eastern Air Command, include Air Marshal Anil Raghunath Nambiar, Air Marshal Rajiv Dayal Mathur, Air Marshal R.D. Mathur and others.

Southern Air Command

AOC-in-Cs, Southern Air Command, include Air Marshal Balakrishnan Suresh and notable AOC-in-Cs include Air Marshal MSD Wollen, Air Marshal Sunderaman Neelakanthan, Air Marshal Rakesh Kumar Singh Bhadauria, Air Marshal R. K. S. Bhadauria, now the Air Chief and others. The list is not exhaustive.

Air Force Training Command

The AOC-in-C, Air Force Training Command is Air Marshal Rajiv Dayal Mathur, Air Marshal R.D. Mathur, formerly of the Eastern Air Command who was preceded by Air Marshal Anil Bhutoria whose wife, incidentally, was Air Force Wives Welfare Association(AFWWA) President.

The Air Officer in Charge, Personnel, is Air Marshal R. J. Duckworth. The Senior Air Staff Officer, SASO, Western Air Command is Air Marshal V. K. Singh formerly SASO, Eastern Air Command while Air Marshal Gurcharan Singh Brar, Air Marshal G. S. Brar is SASO, Southern Air Command formerly SASO, Western Air Command and Air Marshal Inder Jonnalgada Chalapati formerly SASO, Central Air Command is Commandant, Air Force Academy. Last, but not least, Air Marshal Dilip Kumar Patnaik, Air Marshal D. K. Patnaik is SASO, Central Air Command. All these major and minor adjustments to the Air Force were carried out at the height of the Chinese incursions in 2020.

The Navy

The Indian Navy which recently doubled its fleet of aircraft from 250 aircraft to 500 aircraft has three Commands, Eastern Naval Command headquartered at Visakhapatnam, Western Naval Command based at Mumbai and Southern Naval Command, a command which is becoming increasingly becoming pivotal in view of the increasing Chinese presence in the Indian Ocean and the emergence of the Indian Ocean along with the South China Sea and the Pacific Seaboard as a theatre of Sino-American as well as Sino-Indian rivalry. In this connection, Chinese Ambassador to the United States Cui Tiankai, also a former Chinese Ambassador to Japan apart from other countries, said in February 2021 "The United States and China must clearly define their policy boundaries and understand each other's strategic concerns" as America sent warships to the South China Sea under the new Joe Biden administration in a move to flag China. As the United States and China engage in saber rattling and front room and backroom shadow shadow-boxing, in a move that might concern India, it is worth noting that ever since Huang Zhen(not counting Alfred Sao Zu See who served from 1935 to 1937 as Beijing's Ambassador to the United States before the founding of the People's Republic of China), also China's inaugural Ambassador to Hungary, presented his credentials to the President of the United States as the first Chinese Ambassador to Washington after the establishment of diplomatic relations between Beijing and Washington in

May, 1973[soon after the United Nations kicked out Taiwan[which had usurped mainland China's seat in the UN for as many as 22 years](just 13 countries recognize Taiwan now, India not being one of them. Does the United States, known for its penchant to rub China up the wrong way, recognize Taiwan? The answer may surprise many. Not really, with United States Ambassador to Palau (which recognizes Taiwan), John Hennessey Neyland becoming the first foreign dignitary to visit Taipei in the process becoming the first foreign dignitary to visit Taiwan after the outbreak of the novel coronavirus pandemic) and recognized the Peoples Republic of China as the legitimate government of the Chinese peoples.], China's Ambassador to Washington has served an increasingly important role in global politics. Also, the String of Pearls[China surrounding India with bases like the Humbantota[MP Sajith Premadasa] base in Sri Lanka at India's doorstep which India had dismissed as a white elephant while China cashed in on the Indian oversight cultivating the strategic heft aspect and the Ream naval base(its first in South East Asia on the Pacific seaboard), which can house troops and berth warships in Cambodia and the "reverse" String of Pearls theory(i.e. India surrounding China with bases like the Ayni Air Base in Tajikistan and North and South Alagela Islands which it had taken on a 99-year lease from Madagascar keep appearing in the media from time to time. Some scholars note that Sino research in India is pedestrian at best and what can be added to that is that Indo research in China is also loaded. In fact, until recently China did not consider India to be its equal instead calling the United States its main enemy with the United States ending up in its cross hairs and China training its guns on it. However, China traditionally has maintained that India is its rival and competitor, not friend, whatever the traditional Indian efforts to cozy up to China esp. during the Nehruvian era. Many Indian military officers rue the timid approach towards China. However, post 1962 India has become wiser and woken up with the long called for national catharsis occurring and under Prime Minister Modi, new dynamics operate in the Sino-Indian relationship with India giving it back to China with interest in tow esp. during the 2020 armed skirmishes. However, the latest on this front is that there are again rumblings in the Himalayas with China again showing restiveness, this time in Eastern Ladakh and south of Tsangang Tso. In fact, there has been steady attrition of Indian territory, with China quietly chipping away at Indian territory over the years. So, India has to be ever vigilant in this troubled relationship and should not lower its guard. Once Prime Modi had this to say about China which has disputes with over half a dozen of its neighbors, "China reveals a primitive 18th Century mindset, not recognizing national sovereignty and international territorial waters".

Coming back to the operational commands of the Indian armed forces, the Indian Navy is the smallest of the three services having two fleets, Eastern Fleet based at Visakhapatnam and Western Fleet based at Mumbai. The Flag Officer Commanding-in-Chief, Eastern Naval Command is Vice Admiral Ajendra Bahadur Singh who was preceded by Vice Admiral Ajay Kumar Jain who in turn was preceded former CNS or Chief of Naval Staff then a Vice Admiral and now Admiral(retd.) Karambir Singh.

Flag Officer Commanding-in-Chief, Western Naval Command is Vice Admiral Ajay Kumar Chawla and Deputy

CNS is Vice Admiral G.S.Pawar and a former Deputy CNS and Vice CNS are Vice Admiral(retd) Ajay Singh and Vice Admiral(retd) Ajit Singh.

The Indian Navy as of 2021 has 22 frigates, 14 destroyers, 22 corvettes, 1 aircraft carrier (previously it had two), the Vikramaditya(the Russian Admiral Gorshkov aircraft carrier) while a new indigenous aircraft is under construction at the Karwar shipyards, INS.Vikrant and which has since joined service, it had 1 nuclear submarine, the Chakra, which after undergoing damage to its sonar dome while entering Vizag harbor is undergoing repairs at a Russian shipyard. Russia has quoted a whopping $20 billion (Rs 600 crores) as the cost of repair. However, the lease has ended and India won't get the submarine back. The Government has also made it clear it intends to go in for a larger nuclear submarine. Russia was also supposed to have supplied a Akula nuclear submarine with a low radar signature, a Tu-22 nuclear capable bomber and a front winged fifth generation fighter aircraft, the S-37 Berkut for the Air Force by 2010 but these plans seem either to have been shelved or put on the backburner.

The Navy also has the Trishul, Tabar and the Talwar class of stealth frigates. Coming to missiles, apart from the well-known 700 km Agni-I, 2,000 km Agni-II, Agni-III, the 4,000 km Agni-IV India, as is well known created a flutter by cold launching the 5,500 km+Agni-V ICBM whose payload can assign several warheads to a single target, a single warhead can be assigned to several targets and several warheads can be assigned to several targets. China reacted sharply to this saying India could not compete with it in the missile race. In fact, several years back American papers emblazoned the news that India had fired an ICBM, the Surya. Most probably this report is not true or even in the flimsy event of it being true, it is most probably a top class classified secret in Indian Defense Ministry files. However, this is very, very unlikely. When in 1974, India went in for its first nuclear test or even the second nuclear test in Pokhran, Rajasthan in 1997, the Americans pressed the alarm button and alerted their Embassy in Delhi to look out for extra activity in remote areas. India talked of the smiling Buddha and after the second test Pakistan reacted by saying the smile had vanished from the Buddha's face. In relation to a nuclear strike, the press of a button is actually a euphemism for a series of coded signals that end in a nuclear launch.

China has a mixed submarine mix. While on the one hand it has the latest CSS-N3 and CSS-N4 nuclear powered submarines and the Jin class and the Han class submarines which are probably based at the secret Hainan submarine base which China sees as an extension of its Pacific seaboard critical for its OBOR(One Belt One Road) project spanning four continents, Asia, Africa, Europe and Australia which has raised the heckles of countries like India and Germany(as expressed by former German ambassador to India Dr. Martin Ney, present German ambassador to India and Bhutan being Dr.Phillip.A.Ackerman preceded Dr.Walter Johannes Lindner, Walter.J.Lindner), while countries like Morocco(needless to say Pakistan) and Algeria have backed it. For e. g. Chinese ambassador to Algeria Li Lianhe(who was preceded by Zhang Shixian) noted "both countries had fruitful discussions on the Belt and Road Initiative(BRI)" and "these are ties which were built by the older generation under the Comprehensive Strategic Partnership between the two countries". African countries like Morocco and Algeria are backing China's BRI because China has invested heavily in Africa and these small countries do not feel threatened by the dragon's fire. Rather, they have hugely benefited from the Chinese success in Africa which has worked to mutual benefit galvanizing the Chinese economy as well.

China has also bankrolled as many as 29 Third World economies purely for strategic heft and geopolitical leverage. And in the event of a loan default by one of these countries how strong are the Chinese shock absorbers. Indeed, the Chinese have taken a gamble and are on an expansion spree. For e. g. China has acquired bases in Djibouti near the horn of Africa sealed during Djibouti President Ismail Omar Guelleh's (popularly called IOG) visit to Beijing some years back where he met Chinese President Xi Jinping and other Chinese officials. Chinese is also training military officers of the 500 strong Union of the Comoros military. India responded by calling a conference of Indian Ocean Rim Association for Regional Cooperation, now simply called the Indian Ocean Rim Association where Defense Minister Rajnath Singh showed particular interest in Madagascar Defense Minister Richard Rakatoarimanana with whose country India is having a burgeoning defense relationship. Further, India has close ties with the entire grouping of 15 countries bordering the Indian Ocean, a theatre of increasing Superpower and global rivalry. This shows that both India and China are not leaving out the tiniest of tiny countries, as they go about their respective expansion sprees, albeit on different trajectories.

China also has the older Ming class submarine. In one of these submarines, some years back an oxygen leak killed eight sailors. This shows they are outdated and risky.

India also has the French Scorpene submarines, a deal which was signed between then French Minister of the Armed Forces (Defense Minister) Michelle Alliot Marie and Indian Defense Minister George Fernandes after India weighed the pros and cons of the French Scorpene and the Russian Amur class of diesel electric submarines and settled for the Scorpene. These Scorpene submarines are fitted with Indian AIP (Air Independent Propulsion) modules which allow the submarine to remain submerged under water for hours as opposed to earlier generation of submarines which had to snorkel once every 24 hours unlike Pak submarines. Also, recently 4,000 pages of underwater sensors and another 2,000 pages of overwater sensors apart from other classified secrets regarding the Scorpene were leaked possibly into Chinese hands.

Saying the Navy was alive to the threat posed by the dragon, one former CNS Admiral Sunil Lanba noted he found the Chinese submarine deployment in the Gulf of Aden odd. Ostensibly it was for anti-piracy patrols, but the real intent was to spy on Indian and American ships passing through the region. Also, the Indian Navy is doing its own bit of snooping. Some time back Indian Navy radars in Goa tracked a Chinese Soviet-era Sovremenny class destroyer as it passed through the Gulf of Aden through the Indian Ocean on its way to the South China sea. India also recently sent warships to the South China Sea in a bid to flag China apart from cultivating Japan and other countries bordering the South China Sea like Vietnam whose former

President and General Secretary of the Communist Party of Vietnam, Nguyen Phu Trong visited India soon after he entered office upon the death of incumbent President Trang Dai Quang. Former Indian ambassador to Vietnam Preeti Saran who presented her credentials to then Vietnamese President Troung Tan Sang and who was later Secretary (East), Ministry of External Affairs, New Delhi and is now Indian ambassador to the UN Economic and Social Council(UNECOSOC) and whose husband Pankaj Saran is a former Indian ambassador to Russia(immediately before incumbent Pavan Kapoor who is a former Ambassador to first Israel and then to the UAE and holds a MBA from IIM, Ahmedabad and a Masters in Political Economy from the London School of Economics's predecessor, D. Bala Venkatesh Verma, who is a former Indian ambassador to Spain and Dinesh Kumar Patnaik, Dinesh.K.Patnaik is the incumbent Indian Ambassador to Spain) with the diplomat couple playing their due roles in the development of India's relations with Vietnam and Russia in recent times.

India also signed a Strategic Partnership with Vietnam which comes under the immediate purview of Vietnamese Defense Minister Army General Phan Van Giang who is preceded by Ngo Xuan Lich and under the overall purview of Vietnamese Prime Minister Pham Minh Chinh who was preceded by Nguyen Xuan Phuc. Nguyen Xuan Phuc has since become President of Vietnam. The Vice President is Vo Thi Anh Xuan while the Information and Broadcasting Minister is Nguyen Manh Huang. India also has close ties with other countries bordering the South China Sea like Cambodia which Prime Minister Vajpayee visited, Philippines, Singapore, Laos etc. and is an active member of APEC (Asia Pacific Forum for Economic Cooperation). However, India needs to further strengthen its ties with

ASEAN (particularly vibrant Thailand which is economically the third most powerful country in ASEAN and a strong contender for the top position) which is fast emerging as a global Superpower economic bloc, despite Covid-19. China has invested heavily in ASEAN through its former ambassador there Huang Xilian who is now China's ambassador to Philippines.

India needs to do more through its ambassador to ASEAN Jayant Khobragade. Indian ambassador to Cambodia Devyani Khobragade(who came into the spotlight in 2013 during her stint as India's Consul General in New York, albeit in a unsavory manner when she was caught in the soup in a visa scandal involving her maid) should tighten up her boots(and not sort of hang up her boots) and focus on strengthening India's relationship with (if possible, India should acquire a base in proximity to the South China Sea. This will tick off China) Cambodia where, as noted earlier, China has acquired its first naval base in Southeast Asia, a base which can house troops, berth warships apart from having other facilities. To be sure, Cambodia's King Norodom Sihamoni(son of former King Norodom Sihanouk who abdicated the throne in 2004 in favor of his son) and its government led by Prime Minister Hun Sen and prospective heir Mr.Sen's son Hun Manet whom Mr.Sen wants to succeed him through an election and Vice Presidents Aun Pommoniroth, Prak Sokhonn, Ke Kim Yan and Men Sam Yan all of the ruling Cambodia Peoples Party of PM Hun Sen and former Vice President Chea Sim are known India friends although they are now engaging in a fine balancing act between India and China(as evidenced by the Chinese base). And Thailand sent its agriculture minister and Secretary in the Thai government Grisada Boonracchh as Special Envoy to Prime

Minister Modi's swearing-in.

So, India should seize the initiative and work through its ambassador to Bangkok Suchitra Durai and the Thai ambassador to India Patraat Hongtong in developing close relations with Thailand esp. on the economic front. The present Indian Foreign Secretary Vinay Mohan Kawatra's predecessor Harshvardhan Shringla is a former ambassador to Thailand (apart from the United States and Bangladesh). So, he has a personal interest in Thailand. Also, India deployed troops and weapons en masse on to the Chinese and Pakistani borders June 2022 in response to Chinese and Pak troop deployment but there were also some refreshing peace overtures between India and China 2022. But, same year Pakistan supplied high precision Turkish pistols to J&K terrorists for bloodbath and carnage in J&K.

Coming back to the Indian Navy, notwithstanding the latest variant of the Tejas, the Tejas falls short of the Navy's requirements. Former CNS Admiral Sunil Lanba admitted as much when he said, "We are for indigenization, but Tejas doesn't fit the bill." This could be because the forces involved in arrested landings on carrier decks are different in the naval variant than the air force variant. And among a new class of warships that has joined the Indian Navy is the INS Surat. Among the notable achievements of the Navy are the sinking of the Pakistani submarine PNS Ghazi by INS Rajput during the 1971 Indo-Pak War and the sinking of the Portuguese destroyer PRQ Alphonso De Albuquerque by INS Beas during the Goa liberation war. Also, as part of Operation Cactus the Navy was kept on standby during the Kargil War for any Pakistani mischief on the Western Front. And, of course, who can forget the unforgettable bombing of Karachi harbor during the 1971 Indo-Pak War under the able leadership of then Naval Chief Admiral Sardarilal Mathradas Nanda, Admiral S.M. Nanda whose memoirs are titled "The Day Karachi was Bombed" and whose anniversary December 8 is celebrated as Navy Day in India. Although the smallest of the three services, the Navy has always rendered yeoman service in the service of the nation. However, India really needs to go in for a blue water navy as simply because in the words of President Harry. S. Truman "The Navy forms the bulwark of our defense forces as 3/4ths of the world is covered by water". The present Indian Naval Chief is Admiral R.Harikumar.

India's nuclear triad is apexed by the Nuclear Command Authority, Strategic Forces Command and the Andaman and Nicobar Command.

Nuclear Command Authority

The apex Nuclear Command Authority is chaired by the Prime Minister and headed by the National Security Advisor.

Strategic Forces Command

The Strategic Forces Command is the core apex body that oversees India's nuclear triad. When it was formed it was placed under its first Commander, Tej Mohan Asthana. The present Commander is Rajesh Kumar.

The Paramilitary Forces

India's paramilitary forces are the BSF, CRPF, Assam Rifles, Shastra Seema Bal, Indo Tibetan Border Police, CISF and the NSG.

Now let us examine each one in depth. Let us start with the Assam Rifles-

Assam Rifles

Originally called the Cachar Levy in British India, its name was changed to East Bengal Rifles in 1835 and it was not until 1935 that it was named the Assam Rifles. Charged with the task of securing rear lines in the event of war and other principal responsibilities, it is led by an army officer of Lt. Gen. level, and it has seen action during the Congo crisis and in Sudan, Afghanistan, Kosovo and other hotspots and flashpoints of the world.

The various Directors General, Assam Rifles are in reverse chronological order the present Director General Sukhdeep Sangwan, Rana Kapoor, Lt. Gen. Shokin Chauhan AVSM VSM, SM, Ranbir Kapoor, H.S.Karwar, Bhopinder Singh, Lt. Gen. G.S. Katoch, Lt. Gen. Param Bir Singh, Harbhajan Singh, Sushil Kumar, Sidhiman Rai CIE IE the first Director General Mr. H.G. Bartly MC and others.

ITBP

Conceived to be a buffer force between India and China after the 1962 Sino-Indian War to protect the 4,448 km Sino-Indian border the ITBP which has several score aircraft and

50 boats as auxiliary supply the ITBP has also seen action in various hotspots around the world like Sudan, Afghanistan etc. its various Directors General over the years include the present D-G Surjit Singh Deswal, his predecessor Rajnikant Mishra, the first D-G Biswajit Das who passed away 2020, Balbir Singh and others.

BSF

The BSF, whose motto is "duty unto death" has been led over the years by Directors General like the first D-G Khusro Faramosh Rustomji, K.F.Rustomji, Ashwini Kumar, Sharawan Tandon, U.B.Phatak, Suhas Goswami, V.S.Singh, the present D-G Rajnikant Mishra and others.

CRPF

The CRPF has been led by D-Gs like Veerapan slayer Vijay Kumar, Rajeev Rai Bhatnagar, and others. It is among the 7 paramilitary forces of India.

CISF

The CISF has been led by D-Gs like O.P. Singh and others.

Shastra Seema Bal

The Shastra Seema Bal is currently led by Archana Ramsubramanium who was preceded by Surjit Singh

Deswal, S.S.Deswal and others.

NSG

Charged with the task of protecting the Prime Minister, the NSG has been led by Satish Singh, Arun Chadha, Suhas Goswami and others.

RAW (Research and Analysis Wing)

India's external intelligence agency, RAW (Research (gathering intelligence) and Analysis (sifting through it and analyzing it) Wing, whose motto is *Dharmo Dharmah Rakshitah*(in the context of the State, it means that if you protect the State, the State will protect you) and whose notable achievements include the liberation of Bangladesh and the integration of Sikkim into the Indian Union in 1974 has been led over the years by Directors General (DGs) like the first DG *"Kaoboy"* Rameshwar Nath Kao, R. N. Kao, the present DG Samant Goel, his predecessor Anil Dhasmana and others. RAW DG has the rank of a Secretary(R) in the Cabinet Secretariat and is under the direct charge of the Prime Minister.

Intelligence Bureau (IB)

India's internal intelligence agency, IB, has been led by DGs like the present DG Arvind Kumar, his predecessor Rajiv Kumar, ESL Narasimhan(later Chhattisgarh Governor and Joint Governor of Andhra Pradesh and Telangana and

Governor of Telangana), M.K. Narayan, Shiv Shankar Menon(later National Security Advisor, NSA) and others.

Indian Space and Nuclear facilities include apart from India's only nuclear testing site, Pokhran, the Abdul Kalam Island missile testing site near Balasore on Orissa's eastern seacoast, the Satish Dhawan Space Center, Sriharikota, Thumba Equatorial Rocket launching station in Kerala where India began its space quest way back in the 60s with sounding rockets and where Dr. Abdul Kalam personally saw to it that India's space quest succeeded sleeping near the rocket bed sites and the new, latest launch port which is coming up in Thootikudi, Tamil Nadu for which the Tamil Nadu government has already acquired 2,300 acres of land, and score of other space facilities like the Liquid Propulsion Systems Center, Valiamala spread across the length and breadth of India, esp. peninsular India.

It is worth noting, in conclusion, that of the most underated Indians of all time and who deserves far more fame than he has so far got is Indian jurist, Koko Kunsao(Japan's highest civilian honor) Dr.Radha Binod Pal(Jan.27,1896-Jan.10, 1967), who was one of three Asian judges appointed by the UN International Law Commission to go into the "Tokyo Trials" of 55 Japanese POWs including then Japanese PM Hideki Tojo accused of war crimes(crimes against peace) during World War II of whom 28 were Class A "war criminals". Penning a different note, Dr.Pal was the only member of the 11 member jury who in his 1,252 page judgement argued convincingly that not all accused were equally guilty and moved 28 Class A POWs to Class B POWs thus saving many of them from a sure death penalty who would otherwise have been guillotined at the sacrificial altar of the allies's revenge mentality. As the former Indian CJI, Sharad Arvind Bobde, argued "when justice becomes revenge, it loses its character".

Coming back to the Tokyo Trials, Dr.Pal argued, again convincingly, that the murderers sitting in Washington(even Hitler, reportedly, refused to use the far less serious biological weapons during World War II) ignoring all hints of surrender from the spent force that Japan was, and throwing all principles of restraint and neutrality to the winds, killed 2,00,000 people through nuclear bombardment, the aftershocks of which are being felt even today maiming thousands. To add insult to injury, President Obama during his 2021 visit to Japan developed goosebumps and balked at the prospect of apolozising to Japan. To drop his judgement, Dr.Pal was offered the first President of the International Court of Justice but he refused and wrote his judgement. And the Chinese because of their internecine quarrels with the Japanese hate him for his judgement.

A grateful Japan, through its Emperor Hirohito, conferred its highest civilian honor, Koko Kunsao, on Dr.Pal, named two busy roads in Tokyo and Kyotto after him, placed his statue in front of its Supreme Court in Tokyo, opened a research center in his name in Tokyo University and opened a museum and theYasukuni shrine after him. Further, PM Shinzo Abe during a recent visit expressed a desire to meet his family and met his son. Revered in Japan, Dr.Pal remains a much forgotten man in his homeland India.

X

Pakistan

Armed Forces

Coming to the Pakistani armed forces, the 11 largest in the world (Pakistan maintains a force strength far in excess of its size and requirements, mainly because of its India paranoia), the Pakistan Army (its headquarters are at Corps Headquarters, Rawilpindi) which has strategic space unlike the Indian Army (this is because India is a democracy while Pakistan is, at best, a chequered democracy) has 9 principal corps.- the principal ones being at Corps. Headquarters, Rawilpindi, Multan, Quetta, Peshawar and Lahore. The apex Chairman, Joint Chiefs of Staff Committee, is the single point military advisor to the Prime Minister of Pakistan, the Cabinet and enjoys right of audience before the Parliament and the advisement role extends to the Parliament as well as the Cabinet. The post is always occupied by a 4-star rank General, Air Chief Marshal or Admiral.

The current holder of the office is General Nadeem Raza who is preceded by Gen. Zubair Mahmood Hayat (of the Pakistan Artillery Regiment), who, in turn is preceded by Gen. Rashad Mahmood (Pakistan Artillery), Gen. Ashfaq Pervez Kayani (Baloch Regiment), Gen. Khalid Shameem Wynne (Baloch Regiment), Gen. Pervez Musharaf. Gen. Majeed Khan, Admiral Iftekhar Ahmed Sirohey, Air Chief Marshal Farooq Feroze Khan, Gen. Shamim Alam, Gen. Rahimullah Khan, Gen. Iqbal Khan, Admiral Mohammed Shariff, Gen. Mohammed Shariff and others.

The Pakistan Army (the bravest in the world if some reports are to be believed. In any case, small countries are always likely to have brave armies as they have more at stake) which calls the shots in Pakistan, is staffed by Chiefs of Army Staff (COAS) like the present Army Chief, Gen. Faiz Hameed NiM,HiM who commanded the Peshawar Corps. for 1 year. It is mandatory for a prospective Pak Army Chief to command a Corps. level formation for at least 1 year. Other Army Chiefs include Gen. Qamar Javad Bajwa NiM HiM, the powerful Gen. Raheel Sharif (who lost a brother in the 1971 war with India), Gen. Ashfaq Pervez Kayani, Gen. Nizamuddin Butt (only for a few hours), the notorious Gen. Pervez Musharraf who refused to salute the Indian Prime Minister during his stint as COAS and during the latter's state visit to Pakistan and went on to prove his 'mettle', Gen. Jehangir Karamat, also a ambassador to the United States, Gen. Abdul Waheed Kakkar, Gen. Asif Nawaz, Gen. Mirza Aslam Beg, the hatchet man Gen. Zia ul-Haq, the Butcher of Dhaka, Gen. Tikka Khan, Gen. Yahya Khan, and Gen. Ayub Khan (who later became a Interior Minister of Pakistan) and the very first Army Chief, Gen. Frank Walter Messervey.

<u>Pakistan Air Force</u>

The PAF, known for its professionalism and which is the best there is (with even Indian military officers respecting the PAF) is equipped with aircraft like the F-16(peanuts for Gen. Zia ul-Haq, the 'cobra' of Pakistan in the words of Benazir Bhutto), Mirage IV, the 4.0 China-Pak JF-17 which Pakistan is already in the process of phasing out even as India unveils a new variant of the Tejas[the old variant is seen as a sufficient replacement for the ageing Mig-21, a fine aircraft in its time known for its aerodynamics(for e.g. it had delta shaped wings so that the aircraft could rip through the air at routine speeds of Mach 2 or twice the speed of sound) and the mainstay of the IAF] with over 20 squadrons(1 squadron equals 16-18 aircraft, i.e. around 400 aircraft) and an answer to the China-Pak JF-17]. Supposedly, the new Tejas variant will satisfactorily answer whatever aircraft that Pakistan substitutes the JF-17 with. Does India's Sukhoi-30 MKI fighter aircraft stand shoulder to shoulder with Pakistan's F-16? The Sukhoi-30 can destroy buried and doubly buried targets and is a sufficient retort for Pakistan's F-16. Did the IAF shoot down a raiding Pak F-16 during the surgical strikes of 2016? The PAF bought down an Indian Mig-21 Bison and Sukhoi-30 when they intruded into its airspace. India's version that it shot down a Pak F-16 has also been internationally challenged and there remains the further fact that America also corroborated that in their count there was no Pak F-16 missing. The precise facts are as follows:On the fateful night 11 fighter aircraft, both Indian and Pakistani were involved in the dogfight and Pakistan bought down the two Indian aircraft and captured Vikram Abhinandan whom it released with great fanfare later on. However, India held up debris of a

MRAAM(Medium Range Air to Air Missile) that it claimed was launched by the Pak F-16 as "proof" that it indeed had bought down a PAK F-16. This is ominous news for a country like America which is banking on the Indian military to counter China. We can ignore this reality only at risk of underestimating our enemy Pakistan, a mistake Pakistan has all along been doing vis a vis India, to heavy cost. The PAF also boasts of a superior air doctrine as compared to the IAF because of which it will be ruling the skies initially in the event of a war between the two now but will eventually lose the war on account of collapsing ground defenses. Our Army is superior. In fact, not only is our Army not superior, our forces, be it the Army, Air Force or Navy, which rank among the frontline militaries of the world and are second to none, outnumber Pakistan's forces in a 3:1 ratio. This is not patriotism speaking, but reality at work. Because of this reality, although India has, Pakistan, much like the United States during the days of the cold war has not shed its nuclear first use option. But Pakistan forgets it is no United States and cannot hold a candle to India anyday. And what with the prevailing BJP government in Delhi(it seems according to media pundits, there was a paradigm shift in political power from the Congress to the BJP in the long term during the watershed 2014 general election when the BJP finally moved to consolidate its vast Hindu, middle class vote bank(no offence meant to non-Hindus who, contrary to the claims made by the opposition, seem to be in no danger of losing their first class citizen status under the "pariah" BJP. The lack of a satisfactory Prime Ministerial candidate among the opposition parties only goes to help the BJP which the opposition so far has successfully kept at bay, but only so far. A caveat here. The writer, a neutral observer, is no opposition or Congress baiter, or even less a minority baiter with whom all due sympathies are there. But, as Abdul Kalam said, "Facts are facts, whether we like them or not") with its "undercurrent" of "Akhand Bharat" who knows Pakistan may cease to exist in the future as a geographical entity (My due "apologies" to my Pakistani "brothers"). In the world of realpolitik all things are possible both outside and *inside* India where "facts" can be turned on their head and for all we know the Congress-led opposition (Priyanka Gandhi's son Rehan Gandhi(who is now in the Youth Congress)? whom the Congress is preparing for a future onslaught onto citadel Delhi) may pull out a rabbit from under their hat as they spring a surprise in Delhi and seize power. Media "pundits" have been known to come on TV with sheepish smiles before as their poll predictions belied reality.

Coming back to the topic of the PAF, which is tasked with the task of protecting Pakistan's airspace, it has always been led by an Air Chief Marshal of 4-star rank. Only pilots are appointed to this post. The Air Chief is appointed by the Prime Minister of Pakistan pending confirmation by the President of Pakistan.

The various Chiefs of Air Staff over the years in reverse chronological order are the present Chief of Air Staff, Air Chief Marshal Zaheer Ahmed Babar Siddiqi NiM, HiM, SiM,TiM, Air Chief Marshal Mujahid Anwar Khan who is preceded by Air Chief Marshal Sohail Aman, Air Chief Marshal Rao Qamar Suleiman, Air Chief Marshal Tahir Rafique Butt, Air Chief Marshal Tanvir Mahmood Ahmed, Air Chief Marshal Pervez Mehdi Qureshi, Air Chief Marshal Mushaf Ali Mir(born 1934), Air Chief Marshal Kaleem Saadat, Air Chief Marshal Farooq Feroze Khan, Air Chief Marshal Abbas Khattak, Air Chief Marshal Hakeemullah Khan Durrani, Air Chief Marshal Jamal Khan, Air Chief

Marshal Anwar Shamim, Air Chief Marshal Zulfiqar Ali Khan, Air Chief Marshal Zafar Chaudhary, Air Chief Marshal Abdur Rahim Khan, Air Chief Marshal Nur Khan, Air Chief Marshal Asghar Khan, Air Chief Marshal Arthur MacDonald, Air Chief Marshal Leslie William Cannon, Air Chief Marshal Richard Attcherly, Air Chief Marshal Allan Perry Keene. From Leslie William Cannon the rank insignia of the PAF was changed from Commander-in-Chief and again from Tanvir Mahmood Ahmed again the rank insignia was changed, though at a much lower level.

The Pakistan Navy is headed by Chief of Naval Staff, Admiral M.Ahmed Khan Niazi NiM SbT, Zafar Mahmood Abbasi who paid a visit to staunch ally Saudi Arabia in 2020 where he met Saudi Chief of General Staff and Chief of Air Staff Fayyad bin Hamad bin Rawaad al Ruwaili and other Saudi high level military officials and was conferred Saudi Arabia's highest honor, King Abdul Aziz Medal of Excellence. A product of Royal Naval Academy, England of which former English Chief of Naval Staff and First Sea Lord Phillip 'Phil' Andrew Jones is also a product, Admiral Abbasi is preceded by Admiral Mohammed Zakaullah, Admiral Asif Sandila, Admiral Noman Bashir, Admiral Iftekhar Ahmed Sirohey, Admiral Tanvir Ahmed Kanva and others. The first two Chiefs of Naval Staff were Admiral Mohammed Sharif and Admiral Hafiz Hafeez Ahmed (Admiral H.H. Ahmed). The first two Commanders, Pakistan Navy were Vice-Admiral Haji Mohammed Siddiq Chaudhary and Vice-Admiral James Wilfred Jefford. It may be noted here that like in India but as an oppose to their US counterpart, the Pakistani COAS, Chief of Air Staff, and Chief of Naval Staff exercise command over the operational commanders. However, India is contemplating going in for theatre commands(a brainchild of the late CDS Gen. Bipin

Rawat) like in the United States.

National Command Authority

The National Command Authority is the Pakistani apex, nodal body that oversees Pakistan's nuclear triad. Chaired by the Prime Minister, a unanimous decision of the NCA is required to order a nuclear strike. Needless to say, adequate inbuilt guarantees are implicit, never mind the utterances of foot in mouth Pakistani politicians like former Defense Minister Khwaja Mohammed Asif who said at the time the Pak government was contemplating a nuclear strike against India and Railway Minister Rashid Khan.

In addition to all this superstructure, Pakistan also has a Strategic Plans Division which comes under the purview of the PAF. This is an entity peculiar to Pakistan.

The ISI

Pakistan's well known notorious Secret Service ISI operationally responsible for providing critical national security and intelligence assessment to the Government of Pakistan is chaired by its Director General, currently Nadeem Ahmed Anjum who is preceded by Gen. Faiz Hameed, now Army Chief, Gen. Naveed Mukhtar, a product of the elite U.S. Army War College, Carlyle, West Virginia, United States of which former Indian Army Chief and currently Minister of State for Road Transport and Highways and 5-time Ghaziabad MP Gen. V.K. Singh is also a product, Gen. Mukhtar is preceded by a series of DGs like the very first DG, Syed Shahid Hamid who founded the ISI, Major Gen. Robert Cawthome who was responsible for rapidly expanding the ISI, Riaz Hussein, Ghulam Jilani

Khan, Mohammed Akbar Khan, Mohammed Riaz Khan, Aktar Abdur Rahman Khan, Hamid Gul, Shamsur Rahman Kallu, Gen. Ehsan ul Haq, Asad Ahmed Durrani, Ahmed Shuja Pasha, Javed Nasir, Ashraf Jehangir Qazi, Naseem Rana, Muhamad Ahmed, Nizamuddin Butt Mohammed. T. Khan, Gen. Ashfaq Pervez Kayani who went on to become an Army Chief of Pakistan, Rizwan Akhtar, Syed Asim Munir Ahmed Shah and of course Gen. Naveed Mukhtar. A thing that needs to be said here is the Pak military are past masters at emptying American wallets in their fictitious hunt for terror, all of which boils down to Abbottabad. However, of late, the Americans have woken up to Pak deceit as they refuse to buy Pak fiction on terror hunt as they turn off the aid tap. For e. g. America has closed the doors of its elite military institutions like West Point to Pak military officers and here Russia and China are beginning to fill the vacuum left by the West as "new political alignments" take place on the geopolitical field. And Pakistan seems open to buying oil and wheat from Russia in further evidence of expanding Pak-Russian cooperation. There indeed are no permanent friends and enemies in politics and political friends do indeed make for strange bed fellows. And mid-June 2022, former Pak Foreign Secretary Hina Rabbani Khar is leading Pak hard push to get FATF grey tag off as the country tries to hard sell its image as a "soft" state.

Intelligence Bureau (IB)

Founded in 1948, Pakistan's civilian intelligence agency, IB, is Pakistan oldest intelligence agency and its various DGs include Imtiaz Ahmed, Tariq Aziz, Burhanuddin Waheed Ahmed, Ijaz Ahmed and others.

The National Security Advisor (NSA)

The Assistant to the Prime Minister on National Security or simply called National Security Advisor advises the Prime Minister on matters relating to the national security of Pakistan and is the senior official on the National Security Council and the advisement role extends to international affairs and the national security of Federally Administered Tribal Areas and other important issues of national security.

The present NSA is Moeed Yusuf, who is preceded by Lt. Gen. Nasir Khan Janjua, Tabassum Hassan, Tariq Aziz, the infamous Gen. Tikka Khan the first NSA Gen. Omar Mullah and others.

Pakistan Air Bases

Pakistan has around 25 Air Bases divided into Flying Air Bases and Non-Flying Air Bases. Flying Bases are bases off which aircraft operate in wartime and peace time. Flying Bases include-PAF Base Masroor (Mirage 2000 Base), Masroor (Southern Air Command), PAF Base Shabaz(Jacobabad-Pakistan's Afghan springboard, Southern Air Command), PAF Base Samungli(Quetta, Southern Air Command, Tactical Attack Wing), PAF Base Bholari(Thatta, Southern Air Command), PAF Base Faisal(Southern Air Command, Tactical Attack Wing), PAF Base Rafiqui (Shorkot, Central Air Command, Tactical Attack Wing), maximum security PAF Base Mushaf (Sargodha, where Pakistan's F-16s are based and which is Pakistan's most important Air Base, Central Air Command), PAF Base M M Alam(Mianwali, Northern Air Command),

PAF Base Minhas (Minhas, Northern Air Command), PAF Base Peshawar(Northern Air Command), PAF Base Nur Khan(Rawilpindi, Northern Air Command), PAF Base Skardu(for Northern Areas), PAF Academy, Asghar Khan, Risalpur(Northern Air Command), PAF Base Chaklala outside Islamabad, PAF Base Talhar, PAF Base Murid, Murid and an Air Base outside Karachi in Pakistan's Sindh province. These bases are divided into Tactical Attack Wing, Air Superiority Wing, Combat Wing and Air Attack Wing.

Non-Flying Air Bases include PAF Base Korangi Creek, (Korangi Creek, Southern Air Command), PAF Base Malir (Karachi, Southern Air Command), PAF Base Sakesar(Sakesar, Central Air Command), PAF Base Lahore, Lahore(Central Air Command), PAF Base Kalabagh(Nathiya Gali, Northern Air Command) and PAF Base Kalhar(Kalhar, Northern Air Command)

Non- Flying Bases are used for maintenance, air support, training, and mission support.

Pakistani rocket and missile launching stations include the Sonmiani Terminal Launch, Balochistan and Tilla Rocket Testing Site, Jhelum District, Punjab. Apart from well- known Pakistani missiles like the Ghauri, Anza and Haft (Nasr) series, Pakistan has also recently test fired the 2,700km White Falcon (Shaheen III) into the Arabian Sea. Further, it has also tested the Buraq and the Barq pilotless vehicles.

XI

Sri Lanka

Commander-in-Chiefs of the Ceylon Volunteer Naval Force

The various Commander-in-Chiefs of the Ceylon Volunteer Naval Force are in reverse chronological order Admiral D.V. Hunter, the very first Tamil Commander-in-Chief Rajan Kadirgamar, Admiral J.R.S. Brown, Admiral W.E. Banks, and the first Commander-in-chief of the Ceylon Volunteer Naval Force W.G. Beauchamp. The present deputy to the Commander of the Navy, the Chief of Naval Staff is Rear Admiral Ruwan Perera who is preceded by Admiral Ravindra Wijaygunaratne.

The Commander of the Air Force

The Sri Lankan Air Force is commanded by the Commander of the Air Force who is assisted in his duties by the Chief of Air Staff (CAS). The various Commanders of the Air Force include Air Marshal Amal Karunasekhara and others. The CAS include Air Marshal Kapila Bandara Jayampathy, now Sri Lanka's High Commissioner to Malaysia. The various deputies to the CAS, the Vice CAS include the present Vice Chief of Air Staff, Air Vice Marshal WRLP Rodrigo and others.

The Sri Lankan single point military advisor to the Sri Lankan President, the Chief of Defense Staff is the Army Chief Gen. Shivendra Silva, preceded by Admiral Ravindra Wijaygunaratne, Air Chief Marshal Kolitha Gunathilake, Gen. Chrishanta De Silva and others. Incidentally, the present President, Gotabaya Rajapaksa is a former Defense Secretary.

On the topic of South Asia, it is to be noted that Bangladesh imported some diesel-electric submarines from India in mid-2018 and India supplied some Dornier-228 aircraft to Seychelles which will be used by Seychelles for reconnaissance activities. This is not the first time that India has done so. India also helped Seychelles in constructing its new Parliament Annex.

XII
Others

Ethiopian Armed Forces

The Ethiopian Armed Forces or Ethiopian National Defense Force is helmed by a Chief of General Staff, currently General Seare Mekonnen who is preceded by General Samora Yunis. The Chief of General Staff reports to the Defense Minister, currently Lemma Megarsa(once a Prime Ministerial hopeful) who is preceded by Motuma Mekassa who, in turn, was preceded by Siraj Fegassa, Siraj Fegassais(currently Transport Minister). Chief of Air Staff is Brigadier General Yilma Merdassa who is preceded by Air Chief Marshal Molla Hailemariam. Vice-Chief of Air Staff is Air Marshal Michael Teka. Ethiopia had a Navy (with Emperor Haile Selase I as Chief of Naval Operations who was assisted in his duties by his deputy, Vice-Chief of Naval Staff Rear Admiral Iskander Desta) from 1955 to 1996, but with the creation of Eritrea in 1997, it was disbanded. Recently, there was a thaw in relations between warring Ethiopia and Eritrea with the newly elected Prime

Minister of Ethiopia Abiy Ahmed Ali (who at 41 is one of the youngest leaders in the world) visiting Eritrea and meeting Eritrean President Issais Afewerki, also pronounced Issais Afwerki heralding a new dawn In Ethiopian-Eritrean relations for which Mr. Ali was handed over the 2019 Nobel Peace Prize but Mr. Afewerki was deliberately left out of the Nobel Prize citation after an altercation with a woman.

Turkey

The Turkish Defence Minister is Gen.Hulusi Akar, a former Chief of General Staff of the Turkish Army, a infantry specialist like most Army Chiefs around the world and a product of the Infantry School of Warfare who is preceded as Chief of General Staff by Gen.Yasar Guler. Another Turkish Defence Minister is Fikri Isik.

Bolivian Armed Forces

The Air Force

The Bolivian Chief of Air Staff is Air General Marcelo Heredia who is preceded by Air General Ciro Miguel Villegas Ramos, Air General Tito Ganderallas Air General Ciro Orlando Alvarez Guzman, other notable Air Chiefs include Rafael Pabon, Fernando Bilbao Rioja, Ivan Inchauste Rioja, and others.

Bolivian Air Bases

Bolivian Air Bases include La Paz, Cochabamba, Santa Cruz, Puerto Suarez, Cobija, Tarija, Villamontes, Reberalta, Robore, Ouni and Suoco.

Bolivian Air Force aircraft include bombers like the Chinese Hongdu V6, trainer aircraft like the PC 6A Pilatus, Diamond 40C, transport aircraft the C-130 Hercules and C-30 Globemaster and other aircraft.

Defense Ministers include the present Defense Minister Edmundo Novillo, Javier Esteban Riaz who had to put in his papers after a controversy, Luis Fernando Julio Rubio under the previous President Jeanine Anez Chavez and others.

Commanders-in-Chief of the Armed Forces include the present Chief of the General Staff Augusto Garcia, his predecessor Commander-in-Chief Miguel Angel Alberto Garcia, Carlos Sergio Orellana Centallas, William Kaliman under legendary cocalero activist President Juan Evo Morales Ayma whose protege Luis Arce is the current President of Bolivia. The Bolivian President is the Capitan General of the Armed Forces of Bolivia.

<u>Army</u>

Army Chiefs include the present Army Chief Miguel Angel Garcia, Gen. Faut Ramos, Gen. Pablo Inchauste Rioja, and others.

Military Chiefs of Staff include Gen. Emilio Alberto Esteban Rios, Gen. Pablo Arturo Geura Camacho and others.

<u>Navy</u>

The small Bolivian Navy is headed by Chief of Navy Staff Admiral Franz Baldivieso who is preceded by Admiral Orlando Mejia Heredia and others.

How strong are the Bolivian Armed Forces? The Bolivian Armed Forces are rather small with the Army having a strength of around 500 men with conscription being compulsory for those over 18.

Bolivia sources its military supplies from Argentina, Austria, China, Brazil, Russia, the United States, Turkey, Chile, Venezuela, and Ukraine.

Nigeria

The Nigerian Armed Forces are comparatively much bigger. The Nigerian Army is headed Chief of Army Staff (COAS) Gen. Farooq Yahya who promptly replaced Gen. Attahiru Ibrahim who was killed 2021 in a Air Force plane crash that took with it the lives of 10 other Air Force personnel. Other COAS include Gen. Tukur Yusuf Buratai, Gen. Kenneth Minimah, Gen. Lofu Ibrahim, Gen. Mohammed Inuwa Wushishi, Gen. Aliyu Muhammed Gusau who was preceded by Gen. Salihu Ibrahim who in turn replaced Gen. Sani Abacha, Col. Yakubu Gowon, Major General Johnson Aguiyi Ironsi, Major General Sir Christopher Welby-Everard, Gen. William Alexander Mckenzie of the Lanchashire Fusilliers, Major Gen. Foster, and the first COAS Gen. Kenneth. G. Exham. Some of these like Yakubu Gowon, Major Gen. Johnson Aguiyi Ironsi and Sir Christopher Welby-Everard went on to become strongmen Presidents of Nigeria.

Haiti Armed Forces

Haiti's armed forces are headed by President Jovenel Moise who commands COAS the powerful Gen. Raul Cedras who was a one- time President of Haiti who is preceded by Gen. Jodel Lassage and other COAS like the first Army Chief Gen.Demosthenes. P. Xalixte, who was followed by Gen. Antoine Levelt, Gen. Jules Andre, and others. 2020 was supposed to have seen a change in the higher echelons of the Army but it was soon found that it was old wine in new bottles with Army Chief Raul Cedras making a back door entry.

South Africa

With the death in 2020 of South African Army Chief Gen. Thabiso Collin Mokhoso, South Africa saw a new Army Chief Gen. Solly Shoke first Army Chief being Gen. George Meiring. The Chairman Joint Chiefs of Staff Committee is Gen. Lindle Yam.

Germany

The German Navy Chief Vice Admiral Shoensek in remarks made in India said Ukraine cannot get Crimea back, therefore Mr.Putin was worthy of respect and this snowballed into a storm and he had to tender his resignation. Such comments reflect the leftist leanings of many in Germany esp. those belonging to the former East Germany which is why also perhaps Germany has flatly refused to come to beleagured Ukraine's aid[pending the imminent(and now actual) invasion of Ukraine by Russia] and supply weapons to Ukraine forcing countries like Britain and America in that order to take a detour around Germany in supplying weapons to Ukraine and undertaking recon missions. An outreach to those in the leftist constituency of former East Germany? Perhaps. And in a development that is a very, very sobering thought, Germany, in a policy U-Turn, is rearming. For e.g., it has placed an order for American F-35A jets. Indeed, a very, very sobering thought that may have serious implications for the world. However, one swarrow doesn't make a summer.

Italy

During World War II, Mussolini was really a ludicrous figure in European politics and history although the millions of Italians who suffered under him had nothing to be happy about. With typical rhetoric, he committed Italy on the side of Hitler. But, the Mussolini's soldiers were not the disciplined armies of ancient Rome and they had to be extricated from one mess to the other by Rommel's boys in the Africa Corps. But, there is more to it than meets the eye. Reading between the lines and beyond the headlines, experts and those in the know say Mussolini's men were unwilling game partners with the Germans and did not really want to fight against their World War I ally, Britain. So, in 1943 they overthrew El Duce, surrendered to the allies and then fought against the Germans like the Roman Legions of yore.

Poland

The Polish Army Chief is Gen. Rajmund Andresjack and the L-29 Dolphin was the AJT of the Warsaw Pact countries.

Algeria

Like South Africa, Algeria too saw a new Army Chief, Acting COAS Gen. Ali Chengriha who was appointed to fill in the vacancy left by the death of powerful Army Chief Gen. Gaed Salah whose many wars and battles included playing a key role in the Algerian War of Independence against the French.

Israeli Armed Forces

The Israeli Armed Forces which are ever in a state of readiness are apexed by the Chief of General Staff or Commander-in-Chief of Israel Defense Forces presently Raf Aluf(a rank insignia within the Israeli Army) Aviv Kochavi preceded by Rav Aluf Gadi Eisenkot and the inaugural COAS was Chief of General Staff Rav Aluf Yakov Dori. The Chief of General Staff reports to the defense minister currently Benny Gantz of the Blue and White Party who is slated to become the Israeli Prime Minister in October 2021 if all goes according to plan in a power-sharing deal that Mr. Gantz forced upon the wily Benjamin Netanyahu who could manage only a wafer-thin majority in the Knesset. However, things took a different turn and first Naftali Bennet became PM followed by Yair Lapid and soon Mr.Netanyahu was back as the PM.

Israeli only rocket testing site is the Palmachim Air Force Base.

Libya

The Libyan COAS is the omnipotent Supreme Commander Gen. Khalifa Haftar, a former G-O-C -in-C, Eastern Command who consequent upon the internal strife in Libya in recent times(2020s) became the Army Chief.

Iranian Armed Forces

The Iranian Army whose rank insignia includes Artesh, an equivalent of the Indian Jawan, has missiles like the Shahab-3 and the Shahad-4 which Iran tested in the

Persian Gulf. Apart from that amid the intermittent hostilities between Iran and the West led by America in the Persian Gulf, Straits of Hormuz and elsewhere in West Asia are spearheaded by what is basically Iranian rhetoric given the power differential between Iran's naval forces and those of the United States in the region. When America took out the powerful Quassem Soleimani who was responsible for leaving Iran's imprint all across West Asia and elsewhere far beyond Iran's immediate domain and sphere of influence (sure enough oil prices saw a spike with the benchmark Brent crude seeing a dangerous swing upward) in a drone strike in late 2019, he was promptly replaced by a competent deputy Ehsan Qani who until now headed Iran's elite Al Quds force, is the new Islamic Revolutionary Guards(the parent elite force) Commander-in Chief. America, in fact, said Soleimani should have been killed long ago. Anthony Cordesman, Burke Chair at the Institute for Strategic Studies, Washington D.C., however, said "We tend to demonize these people, but they are pretty critical, stable figures" and Michael Knights of the Centre for Near East Policy, Washington D.C. said "Soleimani was replaced by a pretty competent deputy". One has only to remember how the West dubbed former Iranian President Mahmoud Ahmadinejad an "apocalyptic lunatic" to drive home the point that Mr. Cordesman is trying to make. Also, Hossein Salami has replaced Ehsan Qani as the new Al Quds force chief.

Iran's rocket testing sites include the Qom rocket launching site. Iran is also a significant missile power with missiles like Shahab-3 and Shahad-4 behind its behind its belt.

Taiwan

Chief of General Staff

Taiwanese Chiefs of General Staff include incumbent Pei Conwu, Huang Shu Kuang, Tao Chen, the first Chen Li and others.

And, China said it would not hesitate to start war if Taiwan declares war as Taiwan mobilised fighter jets on the Chinese border and took other measures at troop mobilisation. Also, 9 nations including India, US, Japan and Australia and other countries are helping Taiwan build a submarine and stand up to the bully to the North. Three Cheers! to David.

Nepal

Nepal's Army Chief is Gen.Prabhu Ram Sharma.

Bhutan

Bhutan's Army Chief is Chief Operations Officer Major General Gongleon Gogma Bittoo Tshering and he was preceded by Gongleon Gogma Lam Dorjee.

Maldives

Maldives's Army Chief is Major General Abdullah Shamaal and the Vice Chief of Army Staff is Brigadier General Abdul Raheem Abdul Lateef.

Lesotho

The Army Chief of Lesotho, a small country in southern Africa, is Gen.Tefo Mepasela.

And a UN General Assembly resolution was passed for the first time on the fluid situation in Afghanistan condemning the Taliban in June 2022.

Germany's only rocket launching site is the one in the Black Forest while Indonesia's only rocket launching site is the Stasiun Pelunchuran Rocket, Pamuengpuk, Indonesia coming under the purview of LAPAN, the Indonesian Space Agency. Incidentally, two of LAPAN's satellites were launched by India's PSLV rocket which is India's work horse rocket. Iraq has one rocket launching site, the Al-Anbar rocket launching site while Maldives's Gan Island comes under the auspices of NASA.

And the Qaud consists of India, US, Japan and Australia as India, UK, Australia and Japan signed another military pact even as India and Sri Lanka conducted Mitra Shakti, a joint military exercise in Rajasthan in July, 2019. Further, India and Mongolia conducted the Khanjar set of military exercises.

Coming to the Super Weapons being produced by America and other big powers like France that this writer promised to talk about earlier America is producing Super Weapons like the B52Model 12 bomb which is nothing short of a precision-guided miniature atom bomb which in fact was flight tested from a US Air Force fighter bomber that took off from the desert sands of New Mexico. It has maneuverable fins that can be dialed up or down to in order to contain collateral damage and can zero in on any target be it a underground tunnel or a testing site. America also has Super Weapons like the Electro Magnetic Rail Gun

(EMRG) which is something straight out of Hollywood Si-Fi and can fire projectiles which when they hit a person have the effect of a one-ton car hitting a person at 160 mph. Regarding Bill Clinton's pet CTBT, even as America was giving homilies to India on CTBT countries like the United States and France were already violating the CTBT. America with its National Ignition Facility and France with its Laser Megajoule Project. These are scientific experiments designed to create small thermonuclear experiments under laboratory conditions. And not to be outdone in the field of hypersonic missiles by Russia and other powers like China, America April 2022, tested a new type of hypersonic missile adding to its impressive inventory of hypersonic missiles. Justifiably, India's Ambassador to the CTBT Arundhati Ghosh said, "India will not sign the CTBT, not now, not later".

Democratic Republic of Korea (North Korea) Military

Last but not least North Korea. Pyongyang, like its Pakistani counterpart, maintains force levels far beyond its requirement, largely because of its America paranoia which is the North Korean equivalent of Pakistan's India paranoia. Some years back North Korea said, "We can secure a delightful little victory against the arrogant empire of the United States". Now we know where the Iraqi Foreign Minister is! The former North Korean Foreign Minister Ri Yong Ho who has since been replaced by Ri Son Gwon is an expert in negotiations with the United States. North Korea has key allies like China (which is its closest ally), Russia and others. North Korea's principal nuclear testing site is the Samnumdong nuclear testing sites, and its only missile testing site is the Pungye Ri missile testing sites somewhere in north- eastern North Korea. Its ICBMs and missiles include the Hwang (Hwang-I to Hwang-V) series of ICBMs and the Taepodong-1 and Taepodong-2 IRBMs all of which can reach America's Pacific coast and mainland United States which is the main cause for American worry, headache, and anxiety. Some years back a North Korean Unha-2 rocket of the Unha-1 and 2 series exploded and disintegrated over the South China Sea. The engine and fuselage were recovered in the waters off the North Korean coast between Japan and North Korea. The principal US air base in South Korea is the Osan Air Base in South Korea and the principal US air and naval base in the region is the Subic Bay Air Force Naval Base in Japan. North Korea which follows *Juche,* a form of Communist ideology coined by the present ruler Kim Jong-Un's father Kim Jong-iI and has had only three Presidents so far, the present President Kim Jong-Un, his predecessor and father Kim Jong-il and the first President Kim-il Sung has an economy which is in the doldrums and is almost dead as a dodo and what's more imports everything from minerals like mica, manganese to pickup trucks, with internet being banned and with 97% of the roads being unpaved. The North Korean Ambassador to one of its principal allies, Russia, is Sin Hong Chol, a former Deputy Foreign Minister who is preceded by Kim Hyung Sun and others. The North Korean Embassy in Moscow is at 72, Mosfilmokaya Street with the Russian Ambassador to North Korea being Alexander Matsegora. The Russian Ambassador to South Korea is Alexander Kulik and the US Ambassador to South Korea is Admiral(retd.) Harry Bailey Harris, a former Commander-in-Chief of the US Pacific Command (now Indo-US Pacific Command). The South Korean Ambassador to India is Shin Bong-Kil and the Indian Ambassador to South Korea is Sripriya Ranganathan who is preceded by Vishnu Prakash, an expert on South Korean affairs. One former Singapore President Wee Kim Wee who was the first to make use of a constitutional amendment in Singapore's Constitution to prolong his rule is one of Singapore's former Ambassadors to South Korea. As of 2010 the North Korean Secret Service Chief is Kim Yong Chol who is still presumed to be the Head of North Korea's dreaded Secret Service. The Russian Consul General in Chongjin, North Korea is Arkady Ivanovich Lavrov and the Indian Consul General in St. Petersburg, Russia is Deepak Miglani. The Indian Consul General in Vladivostok, Russia is Shashi Bhushan.

The first North Korean Foreign Minister was Pak Hon Yun who was followed by Nam II, Pak Hon Sin, Ngo Dam, and others. The North Korean Foreign Ministry is also presided over by 7 Vice Foreign Ministers some of whom are Song Hyung Chol, Chea Hyung Chol and others. Some of them are experts on European and North American affairs. This in gist all about Northeast Asia, in particular North Korea after separating the grain from the chaff.

KEY TAKEAWAYS

1)The book goes in depth into and analyses the upper echelons of the militaries of more than a score countries including the Big-5.

2)NASA through its Artemis(sister of Apollo and Greek goddess of Moon) will put the first woman and next man onto the Moon by 2025 and establish a sustainable human lunar presence by the end of the decade. The book names the entire list of 21 shortlisted astronauts three of whom will only finally go to the Moon at least one of which will be a woman. And NASA hopes to use the Artemis pool of astronauts to first colonise the Moon and nearby areas and eventually pole vault from thereon to Mars hopefully by the mid-2030s.

3)The book discusses at length the Super Weapons being produced by the SuperPowers and the Big Powers. The book also goes into the space programs of different countries including the space facilities and generally all about man's progress in astronomy.

4)This begs the next question:Are the Big Powers reneging on their arms commitments and taking lesser powers like India for a ride on these.

Yes, indeed, the Big Powers are reneging on their arms commitments. For e.g. countries like America through its National Ignition Facility and France through its Laser Megajoule Project were already violating the CTBT even while doling out homilies to India on CTBT. Which is why India's Ambassador to the CTBT Arundhati Ghosh had at the time said "India will not sign the CTBT not now, not later". That is not all. There are more recent examples. Like for e.g. Russia and America in that order(Yes, Russia has outstripped the United States in the production of Super Weapons) have unveiled a new generation of Super Weapons the likes of which the world has never seen before.